All In

All In

Jerry Yang
with Mark Tabb

MEDALLION
P R E S S

Medallion Press, Inc.

Printed in USA

DEDICATION

To my wonderful wife, Sue, and six children, Beverly Nubqubci, Justice Txujci, Brittney Nkaujnub, Brooke Nkaujntsuab, Brielle Nkaujntxawm, and Jordan Tswvyim. Also to the four most influential people in my life: my father, Youa Lo Yang, brother Cher Xay Yang, Grandmother Pla Her, and Aunt Mee Yang.

Published 2011 by Medallion Press, Inc.

The MEDALLION PRESS LOGO
is a registered trademark of Medallion Press, Inc.

Copyright © 2011 by Jerry Yang
Cover design by James Tampa
Edited by Emily Steele
Photography by Eric Curtis
Shot on location at the Pechanga Resort & Casino®

Published in association with the literary agency of Alive Communications, Inc., 7680 Goddard Sreet., Suite 200, Colorado Springs, Colorado 80920. www.alivecommunications.com

Typeset in Adobe Garamond Pro
Printed in the United States of America
Title font set in Hattori Hanzo

Cataloging-in-Publication Data is on file with the Library of Congress.

10 9 8 7 6 5 4 3 2 1
First Edition

Contents

Prologue
The Longest of Long Shots

"Hey, Jerry? Oh my gosh, I can't believe it's you. I just want to tell you, man, I think you are *awesome,* and I know you're going to win this thing. Wow, I can't believe it's you. Hey, Jerry, if it's not too much to ask, can I shake your hand?"

"May I wash my hands first?" I said to the complete stranger who'd started talking to me the moment I'd stepped out of the restroom stall in the Rio All-Suite Hotel & Casino in Las Vegas.

"Yeah, man, sure. Oh my gosh. Wow. I can't believe I just met the guy who's about to win the freakin' World Series of Poker. Wow." I thought this stranger might pass out right there on the restroom floor. No one had ever been this excited to meet me before.

I walked to the basin to wash my hands. When I turned around, my new biggest fan had a crowd around him.

"Hey, Jerry," one after another called out, "we're with you

all the way, man. You can do it."

I tried to push my way through the crowd, shaking hands as I went. Finally, my older brother and my two brothers-in-law made a path to the door for me.

"Yeah, Jerry. Go get 'em, man," the bathroom crowd cheered.

I'd never experienced anything like this in my entire life. Of all the places in this crowded casino, I'd thought the restroom would be the one where I might find a moment of peace. And after playing poker fourteen hours straight, that's exactly what I needed.

Nine players had started out at the final table at noon on Tuesday, but at two o'clock Wednesday morning, two remained: Tuan Lam and me. We had played so long, with so much on the line, that I could hardly think straight. I knew if the reception I received in the casino restroom was any indication of what lay ahead, I wouldn't have any quiet moments to myself for a very long time.

Making my way toward the final head-to-head showdown, I felt confident. I had a huge chip lead, which made me the odds-on favorite to walk away with the title of World Series of Poker Champion and the huge payday that came with it. However, I knew that in Texas Hold 'Em, chip leads disappear in a hurry. Even so, two weeks earlier when I'd arrived in Las Vegas, no one had counted on me even finishing in the money. I was just one of more than 6,000 poker wannabes. Now I was on the brink of taking poker's biggest prize. I could hardly believe what was happening.

Smiling, I turned to my brother as we walked through the

hallway toward the Amazon Room and the final showdown. "This is crazy."

I couldn't hear his reply.

"Jerry, Jerry, over here, Jerry!"

"How about a picture?"

"How about an autograph?"

"Can I shake your hand, Jerry?"

"How about it, Jerry?"

A huge crowd filled the hallway. So many people called out my name that they drowned out my brother's voice. Pressing against the rope separating spectators from players, they reached toward me as I walked by, snapping pictures like fans at a red carpet Hollywood premiere.

I almost turned around to see if Jerry Lewis or Jerry Seinfeld or some other famous Jerry was behind me, but they were cheering for me: Jerry Yang. On the first day of the World Series of Poker, tournament officials had pulled me aside and asked if I was *the* Jerry Yang, the cofounder of Yahoo. When I'd told them, "No, I'm just a psychologist and family counselor from Temecula, California," they'd shrugged and said, "Oh, sorry to have bothered you."

Now those same officials were giving me the royal treatment as security guards escorted me toward the Rio's Amazon Room. White dots from all of the camera flashes filled my sight.

Patting me on the back, my brother said, "This is for you, Vaam," calling me by my Hmong name.[1] "Enjoy it."

"This way, Mr. Yang." One of the four security guards assigned to me pointed the way to the Amazon Room.

---

1. My parents named me Xao. The day I became a father, Vaam was added to my name as a show of respect in accordance with Hmong tradition.

Calling the warehouse-sized space a room doesn't do it justice. Over the past two weeks, I'd spent so much time in it that I could have made it my permanent address.

As we walked toward the door, I remembered the first time I'd walked in. Over 2,000 poker players had sat in groups of nine around tables as far as the eye could see. And that was only one-third of the players in the tournament. Now, out of all those thousands, two players remained. In a few moments, we would start playing again, winner take all.

"Let me get that for you, Mr. Yang," a guard said. He threw the door open, and I couldn't believe my eyes.

Dead ahead, in the glare of the television lights, sat the feature table, the one where I'd played since noon the previous day. But it looked different.

During the twenty-minute break, tournament officials had stacked $8.25 million in *cash* on the table. The little boy inside of me wanted to run and grab a stack of bills, then thumb through them to make sure they were real.

I wonder if Tuan Lam had the same thought. Like me, Tuan had once been forced to flee his Southeast Asia home to live in a refugee camp. When I'd come to America at the age of twelve, I had one pair of pants, one shirt, and the first pair of shoes I'd ever owned. Now, even if I choked my four-to-one chip lead, I would walk away with more money than my mind could imagine.

How did I get here? I asked myself. *How did I get from the hills of Laos to here?*

"Hey, Jerry," a fan yelled out, pulling me back into the

Amazon Room.

Other fans joined. "Jerry! Hey, Jerry, you're gonna win this thing. Jerry, we believe in you."

So many people cheered that I couldn't understand what they all said.

Then they began chanting, "Jerry, Jerry, Jerry, Jerry . . ."

I couldn't believe it. These people who had never heard of me before I'd made it to the final table now wanted me to win.

I waved, which made them scream even louder: "Jerry, Jerry, Jerry, Jerry . . ." They all looked so happy, as if *they* were about to win no less than $4 million.

Across the room, fans from Tuan's adopted country of Canada waved flags and chanted his name.

It felt like a giant party, not a poker tournament.

I spotted my wife in the second row of the stands closest to the table and tried to get to her.

The fans in the Amazon Room, unlike in the hallway, weren't held back by ropes. Every few steps, I'd be stopped by someone. "Jerry, man, you're the greatest. Would you sign my hat?" A man shoved a Sharpie at me.

Another man pulled up his sleeve. "Hey, Jerry, how about an autograph?"

"What do you want me to sign?"

"Right here. Just sign right here." He pointed to his bicep.

So many people crowded toward me. I signed hats, shirts, poker chips, cards—anything and everything people thrust my way. About the time I thought the crowd was going to swallow me, one of the security guards came to my rescue.

I didn't have much time before play resumed. I had to get to my wife. I needed to touch her, to hold the one person in the room who anchored me to reality before I allowed myself to get swept up in this unfolding dream.

My wife stood and smiled.

I grabbed her and held on, almost breaking down and crying. She and I had come so far to arrive at this moment.

I had spent weeks trying to convince her to drop her objections to my taking up poker for the first time. She worked nights as a blackjack dealer in a casino near our home and had seen too many lives destroyed by gambling. With six kids, a mortgage, and a car payment, the last thing she needed was for her husband to blow his paycheck in a card room. I agreed with her. I didn't want to be a gambler, just a poker player. Who would have expected we would be standing here today?

"Sue," I said, but she couldn't hear me.

The crowd's cheering vibrated the floor.

I placed my mouth next to her ear and shouted, "Pray for me. Keep praying."

I pulled back a bit so I could look at her beautiful face. Her eyes looked so tired. She'd sat in this same spot since the first card of the final table had been dealt, living and dying with me through every hand.

Tears welled in her eyes. She didn't want to cry in front of so many people, but she couldn't help herself.

I wrapped my arms around her. "Don't cry, honey. Don't cry. We made it. Win or lose, we made it. You will never have to work nights again."

Her lips moved as she tried to say something. Even if she could have made the words come out, I wouldn't have been able to hear her.

My mother was standing next to Sue. She's actually my stepmother, but she is the only mother I have known. When I was a little boy in Laos, I'd watched my real mother die giving birth to my younger brother. As I hugged the noble woman I'd always known as my mother, I could tell she was fighting back tears.

In truth, she had little idea what was happening at the poker table. To decipher the action at the table, she had to wait to see who pumped their fists or jumped around. Later, I'd see that the television cameras had caught her raising her hands and shouting, "Hallelujah. Praise God!" a few times. For the Hmong, that is a pretty wild display of emotion.

After hugging her, I stepped over to greet my father. "Well," I shouted, "this is it." I couldn't wipe the smile off my face. I was so happy just to have him here with me.

When I was growing up, my father never allowed me or my brothers or sister to play cards or checkers or chess—or anything that might come close to a game of chance. I hadn't dared tell him I'd started playing poker when I'd entered my first tournament in 2005. And I sure hadn't told him I was going to Las Vegas—Sin City—for the 2007 World Series of Poker after I'd won my seat at one of the casinos near my home. If he'd objected to checkers when I was a boy, you can imagine how he felt about Las Vegas and the biggest poker tournament in the world.

Once I'd survived the tournament long enough to finish in the money, though, I'd called and told him where I was and what I was doing. As soon as he'd heard the words "Vegas" and "poker," he'd handed the phone to my brother and refused to even talk to me.

A couple days later, I'd called him again. By this point, I had played my way into the final thirty-six, which meant I would take home no less than $350,000. This time he'd stayed on the line, but he hadn't believed me. My brother had to go online and show my father the tournament results on a poker website. Only then had Dad agreed to come to Las Vegas to support me.

Standing there looking at my father just moments before the final showdown, I couldn't help but think about all he'd brought me through. Many sons call their fathers heroes, but I have good reason to call my father my hero. He saved my life.

When I think of tens of thousands of my people executed throughout Laos, along with all those who died in Cambodia and Vietnam after the Americans evacuated for good in 1975, I cannot understand why my life was spared. Whatever the reason, it was my father who had made it happen.

We'd come to America, to the projects of Nashville and Kansas City. I'd watched my father work from early in the morning until late at night to support our family. Because he was a refugee who couldn't speak English, he'd had to take the kind of jobs no one else wanted. But he'd never complained. He'd done whatever he had to for his family to survive.

And now my father stood next to me as the crowd cheered

for his son, who was on the verge of taking poker's biggest prize. He seemed so out of place, but then again so did I.

At 5 feet 2 inches, I hardly look old enough to venture inside a casino. Without my dark glasses and the ball cap I keep pulled down low during every poker hand, I looked like some guy who'd wandered in by mistake. One poker magazine reported that after the World Series of Poker I looked like a lost and stunned Scooby-Doo when the villain is revealed. Believe me when I say that based on looks, no one ever mistakes me for a card shark, much less a poker champion.

I looked up at my father and grinned.

He reached out and embraced me, a very non-Hmong thing to do. In our home country, fathers don't hug their sons in public or anywhere else. But on this day, my father squeezed me tight.

I never asked him, but I believe he, too, was thinking about how far we'd come since that day we'd fled our village in Laos.

"Father, will you pray for me? Don't ask God to make me win. But please pray I'll have the wisdom and courage for what lies ahead."

"Of course, Vaam," my father said in Hmong. "I've prayed that same prayer for you every day of your life."

An announcement came through the public address system. My twenty-minute break into reality was over. Pulling my cap low and putting my sunglasses back on, I walked to the table.

"Good luck," I said to Tuan Lam.

"Yeah, you too, Jerry." Tuan shook my hand.

The television lights came up, and the dozen cameras

moved into position.

"Ladies and gentlemen," the public address announcer said, "the final two competitors in the 2007 World Series of Poker are . . . from Canada, with 23 million in chips, Tuan Lam!"

The crowd behind Tuan erupted. Canadian flags popped up everywhere. I thought my eardrums might explode.

"And from the United States of America, with over 104 million in chips, the first man in the history of the World Series of Poker to accumulate more than 100 million in chips, Jerry Yang!"

I'd thought the Canadians were loud. The announcer could hardly be heard. As soon as he said, "the United States of America," more than two-thirds of the crowd in the Amazon Room sprang up and screamed and cheered, the roar quickly evolving into three distinct, repeating sounds: "U.S.A."

Even now, four years later, the hairs on the back of my neck stand up as I remember that moment. No one in the audience that day could have possibly known what those three letters meant to me.

No one, that is, except my family.

Since the day I crossed the Mekong River and escaped Laos, I have not had a country to call my own. Refugees surrender their citizenship the moment they leave their home country. For four and a half years, my family and I barely survived in a Thai refugee camp, hoping to someday find a home.

Even after arriving in America, I'd always felt like an outsider. When I'd come here, I hadn't known the language or any of the basic customs. Other children in the projects had teased me because of the shape of my eyes and my thick accent.

But on this day, Tuesday, July 17, 2007, the country where I'd lived nearly thirty years finally embraced me as its own.

"U.S.A. U.S.A. U.S.A." The crowd kept chanting.

I turned and waved to my new fans, sunglasses hiding the welling tears. Right then I knew, no matter what happened, I had already won more than I could have ever dreamed. For the first time since my early childhood, I was home. From the hills of Laos, across the Mekong River, through the refugee camps in Thailand, to the projects of America, to middle-class life in Southern California, oh, what a long journey I'd made to get here.

Yet this is not a journey I or my family took alone. I am merely one of over 100,000 Hmong who fled our homeland in the Laotian highlands to escape the atrocities the Lao Communists committed against us.

And we are the lucky ones. More than one-fourth of the Hmong population in Laos have been killed since the end of the Vietnam War in 1975.

The war never ended for the Hmong. Because we fought so valiantly alongside the United States against both the North Vietnamese and the Pathet Lao Communist armies, the lives of Hmong in Laos are still in danger today. Human rights organizations have documented the suffering there today as well as the distress of the Hmong still trapped in limbo in refugee camps thirty-five years after the war. All this in addition to the 30,000 Hmong soldiers who died fighting in the secret war for Laos.

I cannot help but think about all of my people as I sit to

write my story. In a sense, this is all of our stories. The name of my people, Hmong, means "Those who must have their freedom and independence." The Communist armies who overran our home in Laos took that freedom away. My story, and the story of all the other Hmong who risked their lives to come to this country, is one of overcoming every obstacle to win our independence once again.

Isn't that the real story of America, too?

In the Shadow of Vietnam

Some people will tell you everything in your life was predestined. Those who believe in God say the Lord did the planning for you. Others blame fate or the gods or karma. The consensus is that your life is set, regardless of what you do or don't do.

My people, the Hmong, have a phrase for this: *dlaim ntawv,* which, loosely translated, means "It's just your luck." Its literal translation carries a heavier meaning: "a piece of paper"; that is, a document on which all the events of your life have already been written out. That means everything has already been predestined, and there's nothing you can do about it. Your path has been set. For those born on a good path, a pleasant life; for those born on a hard road, a lifetime of difficulties until a predestined death.

I don't believe in *dlaim ntawv,* but if I did I might have been tempted to conclude that the paper written out for me contained nothing but bad news. I know that sounds funny coming from a man who caught a lot of lucky cards to win the 2007 World Series of Poker, but it's the truth. I say this because I was born into a people whose history is filled with bad news and difficult paths.

Originally, my ancestors came from China, where we were derogatorily called the *Miao,* a word that basically means barbarian, or *Meo,* which implies slavery. Both words are offensive to my people.

Life was tough enough for the Hmong in China, but it was destined to become even worse. In the eighteenth century, the Chinese emperor slaughtered the Hmong royal family and enslaved most of our people. In time, many Hmong fled for their lives and escaped south to Vietnam, Thailand, and northeastern Laos.

My people settled in Laos, where they carved farms out of the sides of the mountains. When I came along, my father farmed the same way his ancestors always had. With a machete, he cleared all the trees on a hillside. He then piled up the brush in the center of the field and set it on fire. Once the field was cleared, he carved rows onto the hillside, where he planted rice. After a few years, the soil wore out and the field stopped producing a crop, which meant he had to move on to another hillside and start the process all over again.

Dad never owned a tractor or chain saw or any sort of modern tool. Everything had to be done by hand, with machetes or crude axes. The Hmong had farmed like this for generations, and if the world had simply left us alone, we would have farmed like this for generations to come.

But the world would not leave us alone.

My father came into the world at the beginning of the end of the Hmong way of life. During World War II, the Japanese had invaded all of Indochina, including Laos. Hmong warriors fought alongside the French against the Japanese, even though they were not part of the regular army. As the war drew to a close, a new threat emerged. The Vietminh, a group of Communist revolutionaries from North Vietnam led by Ho Chi Minh, invaded. The Vietminh organized a Communist insurgency in Laos called the Pathet Lao. A few Hmong joined the Communists, but most fought alongside the French against the Vietminh and the Pathet Lao. Even though the French pulled out after their defeat to the North Vietnamese in 1954, the Hmong continued defending their homelands on their own.

When the United States took up the fight where the French had left off, the Hmong were right there beside them as well. No one, not the Royal Lao family or the South Vietnamese or anyone in the region, were as loyal to the United States as were the Hmong. As my people say, *dlaim ntawv*: it was just our luck that we chose to ally ourselves with the world's greatest superpower in the one war they were destined to lose.

In 1962, the United States, the Soviet Union, and China, along with the North and South Vietnamese countries and the Royal Lao family all signed an agreement in Geneva that declared Laos a neutral country. Any foreign army in Laos was supposed to immediately exit and allow us to govern ourselves. The North Vietnamese refused to leave. Rather than end the war, the truce actually escalated the fighting. Soon nearly every Hmong man was drafted to join forces against the Communists of the Pathet Lao and North Vietnam.

My father, Yang Lo,[2] was drafted into the Royal Lao Army in 1962. He was seventeen years old. His older brother, Yang La Zang, had been drafted a year or so earlier and was already a lieutenant. After La Zang had joined the army, my father had taken over the family farm for his mother. His father, my grandfather, had died a few years earlier.

No family wants to have two sons fighting in the army at the same time. When my father was drafted, his mother was in a difficult position. With young children still at home, she didn't know how she would keep the farm going. Without it, the family wouldn't survive. The Lao Army was so desperate for soldiers that they drafted the two brothers anyway.

After coming from his small village, my father felt overwhelmed when he arrived at the military base in Phuxe for basic training. You must remember that life for the Hmong had changed little over the centuries. We didn't have running water or electricity, automobiles, or any kind of machinery. Most of us lived in the jungle in bamboo houses with thatched roofs and sustained ourselves by farming and hunting. When my father showed up at the army base with the rest of the new recruits for basic training, he'd never ridden in a truck or seen an airplane up close.

The base consisted of several wooden buildings with tin roofs, dirt roads, and several large fields. A Lao officer herded my father's group into one of the buildings, where another officer handed him a uniform and asked, "What's your shoe size?"

2. The Hmong place our tribal name first, followed by our personal name.

My father didn't know what to say. He'd never worn shoes.

The officer glanced at him, made some sort of sarcastic comment, then shoved a pair of boots at him.

Almost all of the Hmong recruits had the same conversation with the supply officer. Because we lived such remote, primitive lives, the Lao people from the lowlands looked down on the Hmong as nothing but a bunch of dumb hillbillies. Something as small as my father not knowing his shoe size confirmed the lowlanders' suspicions, at least in their minds.

Nevertheless, the Hmong had always been strong warriors, and our jungle survival skills made my people the perfect guerrilla fighters. The Lao royal family desperately needed us in the war effort to survive the onslaught of the Communist armies.

After receiving uniforms, my father's group was herded to a large field in the middle of the base. A platform had been set up on one end. General Vang Pao, the great Hmong military leader, walked out on the platform and gave a brief speech welcoming the new draftees into their grand struggle for freedom against the Communists.

The general had barely finished talking when a Lao Army officer marched out and started barking orders. Other officers began directing the draftees to different parts of the base. My father's military training was already in high gear.

A few of the officers were Hmong. Others were Lao and Thai. Walking amongst all of them were the first Americans my father had ever seen other than the missionaries who'd visited his village.

No matter who barked orders, my father knew who was

really in charge of the camp. These Americans didn't wear military uniforms but were CIA officers. My father didn't know it at the time, but he'd come into the army at the moment the CIA had decided to launch full-scale guerrilla and counterinsurgency operations to try to drive the North Vietnamese out of Laos.[3] As luck would have it, my father and the rest of the Hmong serving in the Lao Army were the foot soldiers assigned to carry out this strategy.

Basic training consisted of learning to shoot a military rifle, to throw hand grenades, to load and unload ammunition, and to set traps for the enemy. All the while, in the distance, the trainees could hear shelling from fighting between Pathet Lao and Hmong soldiers.

Even though my father was officially part of the Royal Lao Army, the Hmong were never considered regular army. Drill instructors didn't waste time trying to teach him and the other Hmong how to march or anything like that. Instead, every day consisted of new lessons on fighting and surviving under extreme conditions.

About the time my father had acclimated to the army base, the training ended. General Vang Pao needed soldiers right away. After sixteen days of preparation, my seventeen-year-old father was declared ready to fight.

When it came time to ship out, my father asked if he could be assigned to the platoon of his brother, La Zang. General Vang Pao granted his request. *Dlaim ntawv.* It was just his luck that this would send him to some of the most brutal fighting of the war.

Under the direction of the CIA, General Vang Pao sent

---

3. Jane Hamilton-Merritt, *Tragic Mountains: The Hmong, the Americans, and the Secret Wars for Laos, 1942-1992* (Bloomington: Indiana University Press, 1999), 123.

my father's unit behind enemy lines to the infamous Ho Chi Minh Trail, the primary supply line for the North Vietnamese troops fighting in South Vietnam. Without the Ho Chi Minh Trail, the war in Vietnam would probably have ended in a matter of months. Almost the entire path ran through Laos and Cambodia. As far as the Hmong were concerned, stopping the flow of supplies from North Vietnam to South Vietnam did nothing to help drive the Communists out of Laos. However, because the United States had asked General Vang Pao to send troops to attack the North Vietnamese along the trail, that is exactly what he did.

My father had no idea where he was going when the orders came to ship out. Before that, he had pulled his brother aside. "No matter what happens, La Zang, I will not leave your side. If we are meant to die, we die side by side."

"Absolutely, we are in this together to the very end."

While this may sound overly dramatic to some Western readers, the Hmong and Lao armies were not like the American military. When fighting grew fierce, or when men went down with injuries, the situation often degenerated into every man for himself. If you didn't have a close relative watching out for you, you didn't survive long.

My father and La Zang had not only each other but also the privilege of serving with their uncle, a longtime army veteran who'd fought alongside the French against the Japanese during World War II.

On the night my father's basic training ended, several American helicopters dropped into the training base.

"This is it. Let's go," La Zang yelled to his platoon. "Everyone, grab your gear and follow me."

My father grabbed his M-1 and small pack and took off after La Zang, who was in a dead sprint toward one of the helicopters. Their unit jumped in and took off.

Throughout the flight, my father closed his eyes and prayed. Two weeks removed from a stone age village, he now flew over the jungle, headed straight east. He'd never even ridden in a car, let alone a helicopter.

A short time later, the chopper dropped.

"Go, go, go," La Zang yelled.

When they landed at the primitive base camp, my father had never been so glad to see solid ground. La Zang gave their unit eight hours to rest and eat.

It would be the last time my father would sleep for another two days.

My father's first mission as part of an elite guerrilla fighting squad of twenty soldiers set the tone for his four years in the army. His platoon was ordered to go to a hill overlooking the Ho Chi Minh Trail and wait. Communist soldiers were supposed to come down it sometime that day, most likely in the morning.

"Our instructions are simple," La Zang explained to his platoon. "General Vang has ordered us to keep them from reaching their destination no matter the cost. Get some rest, brothers. You'll need it."

The platoon marched a full day and night through the jungle to the rise overlooking the trail. My father spent the entire time praying to God and to his ancestors for protection.

His prayers were answered. The unit managed to reach its destination without being fired upon.

As they waited for the enemy to arrive, they rested to regain their strength.

A heavy fog hung over the valley below. They could hardly see anything. A rumbling sound came from a distance.

La Zang stood, motioned to his unit, and passed the word: "It's time."

They attacked, taking the Communists by surprise. A fierce fight ensued. My father and uncle's platoon inflicted a great deal of damage on the enemy and drove them back.

Grenades filled the air. Explosions went off all around my father, who would later call it the worst day of his life. All around him, Hmong soldiers lay wounded or dead. He came upon one soldier whose face had been blown off. Other men lost arms and legs to land mines and mortar shells. He had never witnessed so much death.

The worst was yet to come.

My father looked over just in time to see an explosion knock his brother to the ground. Fearing he was dead, my father rushed to him.

La Zang was alive, but the shrapnel from the grenade had cut into his stomach. Medical tests would later show that his large intestine had been cut in three places.

My father knew his brother would die without immediate medical attention.

When the Communists retreated, my father and great-uncle

picked up La Zang and joined the platoon heading back toward the base while a couple soldiers fell back and set booby
traps to keep the Communists from following.

About an hour later, my father heard the grenade booby traps
exploding behind them. They were being chased. Though the
platoon picked up their pace, the Communists closed the gap.

Finally, my father's platoon reached a place in the highlands
where the trail narrowed between jutting rocks overlooking a
cliff. All the while, they could hear the Communists gaining
ground. To have any hope of escape, they had to take the trail.

"That's it," one of the soldiers said. "We can't carry your
brother any longer. He's slowing us down. If we don't leave
him here, we'll all be caught and die."

La Zang turned to my father. "They're right. I've lost so
much blood I probably won't make it. Leave me. There's no
need for all three of us to die here."

"No, Brother, I won't do it," my father said. "I will never
leave you behind."

Then my father and his uncle walked to the path through
the rocks, blocking the platoon's path of escape. The two of
them raised their guns, and my father declared, "If I have to
die to save my brother, then so be it. But know this: we will not
leave him behind. If you refuse to help him, it will not be the
Communists who kill you. I will. If he dies, we all die."

Seeing the look in my father's eye, the other soldiers knew
he and his uncle were serious. My father was prepared to fight
against his entire platoon to save his brother.

"Okay, okay," the other soldiers said, "we will not leave La

Zang behind."

They managed to get through the rocks without getting caught. The Communists stopped their pursuit but radioed ahead to others in the area.

While mortars rained on my father's platoon, they raced for one whole day and night to make it back to their base. My uncle survived, but two others from the platoon were killed by the mortar attacks.

Sadly, a few years later, after my father left active duty, La Zang was captured by the Communists. Along with his entire family, he disappeared into a Pathet Lao reeducation camp. My father would not see him again for thirty years, when we were able to locate him and bring him safely to the United States.

That first mission set the tone for the rest of my father's time in the army. Over the next few years he fought, often going days without sleep, always surviving on little food or water. Most of the time, he lived on whatever he could find to eat in the jungle. He slept in ditches and foxholes, in downpours and blistering heat.

At one point, he pulled off his wet boots and found his feet had turned white from the nonstop rain. He thought he might develop trench foot or gangrene if he didn't take the time to let his boots and feet dry out, but the constant shelling kept him moving on.

As luck would have it, one mission my father barely survived would later help save his family. In 1963, my father was stationed in a base that overlooked a valley. The Hmong controlled the mountains on one side of the valley, the Communists the other. Day after day the two sides lobbed mortars and exchanged machine gunfire.

The Hmong depended on American cargo planes for their supplies. The planes didn't land but instead dropped the supplies by parachute to the men below. Most Hmong platoons received their supplies this way.

One day my father heard a huge explosion in the sky. Everyone looked up and noticed a cloud of smoke where an airplane was supposed to be. A few minutes later, a call came through the radio reporting that an American plane was down.

"Get your platoon and go find any survivors before the NVA get to them," the commanding officer told my father.

Just as his first mission at the Ho Chi Minh Trail had been, rescuing the American pilots was easier said than done.

The cargo plane crashed on the far side of the valley near the mountains controlled by the North Vietnamese Army. Hostile soldiers, booby traps, and land mines were positioned between my father's platoon and the downed pilots. On top of that, artillery fire continually rained on them. Nevertheless, my father did not once question the order.

From the day the first American airplane was fired on while flying over Laos, Hmong guerrilla fighters had fought and died to save them.

My father's platoon took off through the jungle in the dark. Six hours later, they came upon the crash site. No one was there. The Americans were gone. The platoon spread out and searched the immediate area. "*Tahaan* Vang Pao," they called out, translated "Vang Pao's soldiers," as they searched the area for parachutes and survivors. Finally, they came upon a man hiding behind a rock near a small stream, a makeshift white flag in one hand.

"Vang Pao," my father called out.

"Vang Pao?" the man said.

"Vang Pao, yes," my father said, using the one English word he knew.

From behind a rock, the American pilot stood up and cautiously walked toward my father. Dried blood covered the side of his face, but none of his injuries appeared to be life threatening.

"Others?" one of the men in the platoon asked.

"No, no others," the pilot replied. "They are all dead."

My father's men didn't speak much English, but they understood the word "dead."

"Quickly, come with us," my father said in Hmong and motioned for the pilot to follow them. The men in the platoon surrounded the pilot like Secret Service agents around the president as they hiked back through the maze of booby traps and land mines toward their camp.

As soon as they arrived, a helicopter touched down at camp. They shoved the pilot inside, closed the door, and watched the helicopter fly him away to safety. My father never learned the pilot's name, and few records were officially kept of such rescue operations, but one thing was certain: the pilot was safe.

My father was on to his next mission.

Even with all that my father went through in the war, *dlaim ntawv*, it was not his destiny to die. After six years of active service, most of which were spent behind enemy lines, my father put in a request for discharge.

During one of his sporadic leaves, he'd married my mother. It was, like most Hmong marriages, arranged by their two families. My grandmother had selected my mother for my father. The couple had grown up in the same village, yet my father had never thought of marrying her. After all, she was seven years younger. However, the families had other ideas. My grandmother paid the dowry to my mother's parents, and the marriage was sealed. By the time my father requested a discharge, my oldest brother had been born.

At first, needing every able-bodied Hmong male to fight, General Vang Pao denied my father's request. Six months later, my uncle, who'd now been promoted to the rank of captain, convinced his superior officer to grant my father's request. It didn't hurt that my mother and the commanding officer were related.

Not long afterward, I came along.

My father remained a soldier even though he wasn't with his platoon any longer. Our village was 40 miles from the front lines, and my father was in charge of its defense.

For as far back as I can remember, I heard cannons and bombs and gunfire. Some nights, the blasts sounded as if they were directly outside our house, even though they were miles away. I would lie awake, fearing the moment the Communist soldiers would storm our village and kill us all.

From a very young age, I knew what they'd done to other villages. I'd overheard my father's stories of what he'd seen when his platoon had come upon a Lao village after the Communists had come through. I didn't know exactly what the word "rape" meant, but I knew it was a very bad thing the Communists did to the women of the villages they overran. And I heard how babies were bludgeoned, children's abdomens were split open, and men were forced to watch their families suffer before being killed themselves in the most gruesome ways.

As our uncle and father had, my brother and I made our own pact. If the Communists invaded our village, Xay and I would fight together until the very end. We may have been little boys, but that didn't stop us from practicing the kung fu moves we were determined to pull on any soldier foolish enough to threaten us. We practiced punching and kicking and screaming. We joked about how, if that didn't work, we'd shoot them down with our slingshots, like David against Goliath.

I know my father must have seen his two sons jumping around like Jackie Chan, but he never laughed at us. Instead, he took us into the jungle on hunting trips. There, he taught us which plants were edible and which were poisonous, how to trap small animals, and all of the other survival techniques he'd mastered over the years.

I didn't realize it at the time, but my father was preparing my brother and me for the day the soldiers would invade our village. He knew it was simply a question of when, not if, my nightmare would come true, yet I never saw even a trace of fear in him.

Not only did my father train my brother and me, but he also used to pull the men of our village together and train them in the basics of warfare, using the handful of guns we had in our village. As I mentioned, he knew what was coming. After all, *dlaim ntawv*, we were destined to live at the time when the Hmong way of life came to a horrific end.

2

The Hmong Tom Sawyer

Growing up in Laos, I was always hungry. It wasn't that my father couldn't provide. He was a farmer and a very good one at that. He was also an accomplished hunter, one of the best in our village. Even so, when I think of Laos, I think of hunger. No matter how hard my father worked, life in Laos seemed to fight him.

I will never forget one particular day when I went with him to our farm. As we got close to the fields, I heard a strange buzzing sound. Even now, over thirty-five years later, I can still hear that sound ringing in my ears. I never heard anything like it before or since. It had such an otherworldly quality that I wondered if my life was in danger.

I didn't want to get any closer to the sound, but my father did. He picked up the pace and nearly sprinted up the hill to our farm just over the rise. Not wanting to be left by myself, I ran after him. The closer we came to the farm, the louder the sound became. My ears ached from the intense buzzing.

As we topped the hill, I looked at our farm and couldn't believe what I saw. All of our rice plants had changed color and appeared to sway in a way that wind could never cause.

"What is it, Father?"

He didn't answer, which frightened me more than anything he could have said. He ran down the slope toward our rice fields and began swatting. With each swat, the heads of the plants appeared to rise, then settle back as soon as my father passed by.

I ran after him. Only then could I see that the plants themselves weren't moving; insects were. Our rice field had been transformed into something like one of the plagues on Egypt from the Bible. All around me, grasshoppers were piled on the heads of our rice plants. And their sound? It was more than a buzzing. They *crackled* as their bodies banged against one another, *crunched* as they chewed on our plants, and *sucked* the milky sap out of the plants, the sap that was just days away from hardening into grains of rice.

I tried to keep up with my father. Grasshoppers popped under my bare feet. I looked up to a sky that seemed to be filled with huge, greenish-gray swirling clouds. Grasshoppers had contaminated the entire valley. More and more descended on our field.

"Father," I called out. I was afraid. At the same time, as strange as it seems, I was a little relieved. In my young mind, I thought, *They're just bugs. At least my life isn't in danger.* How little I understood.

My feeling of relief dissolved as soon as I caught up with my father and saw something I never had before: tears ran down his cheeks. Hmong men don't show emotion, and they *never* cry.

Then my father began to pray, but this was a different kind of prayer than I'd heard him say. He cried out with a voice that broke my heart, "God, why did You let this happen to my family? You know how hard I worked. What are we going to eat now?"

My father knew, just as I was about to learn, that we couldn't simply plant more rice. In Laos, the planting season falls into a narrow window in the spring, which was long past. The grasshoppers had consumed all of our rice for the year.

Later that night, my father had to break the news to my mother. It had to be the hardest thing he had ever done.

Other villagers came to our house and pointed at him, demanding, "What are we going to do now?"

My father wasn't just a farmer. He was also the chief elder and pastor of our village. Unlike in most Hmong villages, all but two families in ours were Christians. My father wasn't the only one wondering why God had allowed this to happen.

As the men asked my father what to do, the women wailed. Hmong people make a certain cry after a death. Even though no one had died, I heard the sound that night and it terrified me. My imagination was probably running away with me, but I felt extra hungry as I tried to go to sleep.

The next day, no one cried. No one asked my father what to do. Dwelling on how our rice crop had flown away in the bellies of thousands of grasshoppers wouldn't give us anything to eat.

Within a matter of weeks, our rice supplies ran low. My father responded by spending more and more time hunting in the jungle. We ate whatever he killed and brought home. I remember eating everything from deer, wild boar, and game birds to monkeys, gophers, porcupines, and even rats. When you're hungry, you eat what you can find.

My father also continued to show my brothers and me how to find edible roots and leaves in the jungle. The days we stumbled across bamboo shoots were the best.

By not panicking but doing what had to be done, my father taught me a valuable lesson. I learned to never give up, to never lose hope, to never allow my circumstances to rule me. This positive perspective would give me strength in the years ahead.

The difficulty of life in Laos didn't stop me from finding ways to have fun. And my idea of fun almost always involved mischief. I'd never heard of Mark Twain, but I was the Hmong Tom Sawyer. Other kids contented themselves with kicking around an inflated pig bladder that passed for a ball. I enjoyed that as much as they did, but I also liked climbing high up in a tree and—how do I put this delicately?—relieving myself on the unsuspecting people below.

Since my father was the village leader and pastor, the victims of my pranks yelled and screamed not only at me but also at my father, a man who should have been able to control his wild son. At least that's what they told him, and that's what he told me as I bent over for the regular spankings I knew I deserved.

No matter how hard my father tried, lectures and spankings

could not drive the Tom Sawyer out of me. I simply had too many ideas of fun and exciting things to try, and my small gang of friends was always eager to do whatever I suggested. None of them ever stopped and asked, "Hey, Xao, do you really think that is such a good idea?" I wish they had.

One Saturday afternoon, when most of the people of my village were off working on their various farms, my buddies and I carried out the single worst idea I'd ever had.

For some odd reason, I thought it would be fun to get some big sticks, climb up into the community chicken coop, and smash all the eggs we could find. For a boy who was always hungry, smashing eggs was a foolish thing to do. Unfortunately, my seven-year-old brain didn't think that far ahead.

I was the first one to climb into the coop, stick in hand. The chickens barely stirred when I stepped in and hardly knew what to do when my stick came down with a loud *pop!* on the eggs in the first unattended nest. *Pop!* Another egg. Then another. And another. My buddies joined in, and eggs popped everywhere.

Soon the chickens caught on that something was amiss, which sent them all squawking and flying around the coop. From time to time, I had to shove a stubborn hen off her nest, then—*pop! pop! pop!*—the eggs burst. Yolks, feathers, and hay filled the air as we rushed around, popping eggs as fast as we could. By the time we were done, my buddies and I were covered from head to toe.

Since we left yolk-covered footsteps down the coop ladder and all the way back to our hideout, my father didn't have to call in the village CSI team to figure out what had happened.

As I recall, my father had to pay the chicken owners for their lost eggs, and I could hardly sit for a week.

The great chicken caper was still fresh in the villagers' minds a couple of months later when my great-uncle returned home from church and discovered his prize pheasant dead in its cage.

Even though this man was my grandfather's brother and my great-uncle, we all called him Grandpa as a sign of respect because, though he was probably barely over fifty years old, he was one of the oldest men in our village.

Now, one dead bird may not seem like much, but this was a serious offense in my village, where we relied on hunting for food. Grandpa specialized in hunting game birds and used this pheasant as a live decoy. To him, this wasn't just any bird. He treated it better than he did his own children. Because this pheasant was such a valuable possession, he hung its cage in a place of honor on his porch.

According to Grandpa, this bird had been alive and well when he'd left for church that morning. When he returned, he found it lying in a heap in such a way that indicated it had not died of natural causes.

As soon as Grandpa discovered his dead bird, he grabbed the cage and went straight to my father.

As the chief elder of the village, my father was the one everyone brought their problems to. That's all I thought was going on when I saw Grandpa, his wife, and their two adult sons storming up the path to our house.

Every time a villager came to my father with a problem, I always tried to position myself near him to listen in. I admired my father's wisdom and wanted to learn from him, which is why I didn't run away when Grandpa came to see us. Little did I know that my curiosity would get me into trouble once again.

Grandpa and his sons were visibly angry but kept themselves under control.

"All we want to know is who killed our bird," Grandpa said. "It had to be someone who was not at church today, because, clearly, that's when they killed it." And then he said something that made my heart jump a beat. "I noticed," he said as he turned toward me, "that Xao and his friends were not at church today."

As soon as Grandpa said this, my father turned to me and looked me in the eyes. "Xao, did you miss church today?"

Unfortunately for me, I had made the mistake of choosing this particular Sunday to skip church and spend the day looking for sweet adventure in the jungle.

The closest thing we had to candy was a certain fruit that grew wild not far from our village. According to my calculations, it was about time for it to be ripe. I'd come up with a brilliant plan for my gang to skip church and spend the day gorging on fruit.

As always, my buddies had gone for it. As it turned out, the fruit wasn't ripe, so we went to the river and spent the day swimming and playing with marbles we carved out of rocks.

Since church was pretty much an all-day affair, we managed to get home before it let out. No one noticed we'd been missing.

Or so I thought.

"Xao, I asked you a question. Were you in church today?"

I swallowed hard. "No, sir. I was not." I knew what was coming.

"Xao," my father said again with that tone that melted my spine, "did you kill Grandpa's bird?"

"No, sir."

"Did you witness one of your friends killing the bird?"

His look filled me with dread. "No, sir."

"Do you know anything about the death of Grandpa's bird?" His tone was growing increasingly stern.

"No, sir. My friends and I spent the day at the river. We'd planned to go collect some fruit, but it wasn't ripe, so we went to the river instead. We returned home right before church let out."

"But you broke all those eggs a few weeks ago."

My heart sank. "I know, sir, but we did not touch Grandpa's bird."

Grandpa exploded. "This is ridiculous. How can you believe anything this boy has to say? I know he and his little band of thugs killed my bird."

All I could think was, *Xao, you picked a very bad day to skip church.*

I guess Grandpa could tell my mind was wandering because he leaned down, got right in my face, and screamed, "You tell your father what you did, you terrible boy."

My father immediately chimed in. "Xao, if you did this, just tell me and everything will be fine."

He may have said everything would be fine, but I knew it

wouldn't be for me or my backside. I stood there, silent. Tears formed, but I refused to let them fall.

Grandpa continued yelling and cursing, with his two sons chiming in.

Word of what had happened spread through the village, and everyone rushed to see what the commotion was about. I guess the growing crowd made my father think he needed to end this as soon as possible, so he sent my older brother to round up the rest of the members of my gang.

I can still picture the way they looked as they came walking in my house, their heads hung low, hands folded as if they'd been handcuffed.

To me, they looked scared; to the gathering crowd, they looked guilty. People yelled, "All the culprits are finally here. We can tell you're guilty." People even yelled things about the chicken coop caper. Then someone yelled, "Teach them a lesson," which we all knew meant a sound beating.

Now that all the delinquents were together, my father reached into the rafters and took down the bamboo stick my brothers and I were all too familiar with. He slapped it against a hand, and my buddies' eyes grew wide as saucers. "Okay, Xao, this has gone on long enough. Tell me the truth. Did you kill Grandpa's bird?"

My friends turned to look at me. They knew if I cracked and confessed to something I hadn't done, they'd be punished right alongside me.

I looked my father in the eye, thinking, *He doesn't believe me.* That upset me more than anything else. By raiding the chicken coop, I had lost my father's trust. "No, Father, I am telling you the truth. I did not do it." I spoke with all the sincerity a seven-year-old could muster.

I don't know whether he believed me or not, but with eyes full of anger and frustration, my father turned and walked the line to each of my buddies. "Did you kill this bird?"

My buddies were so frightened that they could barely speak. Their answers came out in weak whispers no one could hear. The pathetic sound made me want to laugh, but I stopped myself. It would've been very bad timing.

"Speak up. Give me an answer. Did you kill this bird?" my father yelled.

Even more frightened now, they gave the same answer. "No."

With each denial, Grandpa and his sons became more upset. "Why are you wasting your time asking questions of liars? Do what you know you must."

"I am not going to waste any more time with you boys," my father said. "Tell me right now what happened to that bird."

Even though we were innocent, the pressure to confess was overwhelming. My buddies could not move. I think if this had gone on much longer, they would have cracked.

I spoke up for all of us. "Father, I swear to you, we didn't have anything to do with killing that bird."

This sent Grandpa over the edge. He was determined to get a confession out of us, and he knew the way to do it. According to Hmong tradition, two simple tests will determine the guilt or innocence of a person accused of a crime. In the first test, the village elder takes a bowl of cold water and kills a chicken over it, catching the chicken's blood in the water. As he kills the chicken, he pronounces a curse over the bowl. The accused must drink the water. If he's guilty, he will die in a matter of weeks. I'd never heard of this until Grandpa demanded my father perform the test right then and there.

"Dear Grandpa," my father said, "remember we are talking only about a dead bird."

Grandpa seemed to soften a bit. "Well then, we should use the oil." As Grandpa explained it, the second test of guilt or innocence involved dipping the finger of the accused into a pot of boiling oil. "We've done this many, many times," Grandpa tried to reassure me, "and it always works. If you are innocent, the oil cannot harm you. But if you are guilty . . ." His voice trailed off.

When my father hesitated, Grandpa pounded the table, pointed at him, and said, "You are our leader. It doesn't matter that this is your son. You must do what's right by the village."

I could tell by the look in my father's eyes that I was in serious trouble. He was a fair man, but he was also a wise man. He would much rather have spanked me with a bamboo rod for something I hadn't done than take the chance of having me severely burn my finger. Bruised bottoms heal much faster than deep-fried fingers. I don't think he had any more faith than I did that the oil could prove one's innocence, which led me to believe that he would go ahead and punish me to get this over with.

Xao, I said to myself, *you'd better do something now.*

In Hmong culture, children don't address their elders unless they're spoken to, but this was an extreme situation. "I agree, honorable Grandpa," I said, "that the test of the boiling oil is the best way to prove my innocence."

My father looked shocked, and Grandpa seemed to calm down a bit. Both must have thought I was crazy.

Before either could say a thing, I quickly added, "However, I have never seen the test of the oil, and neither have my friends. I want to make sure it works before I submit to it." I looked straight at Grandpa. "Therefore, because we know you are completely innocent in this matter and you most certainly didn't harm your own prize pheasant, I ask that you dip your finger in the oil first. Once I see that the oil cannot harm an innocent man, I will be next in line."

"How dare you speak to me like that?" Grandpa screamed in response. "How dare you challenge me?"

I'd only thought he was angry before. He began flailing his arms and yelling so that everyone in the entire village could hear him. "You are an insolent, lying, horrible little boy. I will show you what we do to children like you."

I ducked just a bit, anticipating the blows I thought were coming.

"Dear Grandpa," my father interrupted, "I too have never seen the oil test. I would also like to know that it works before my son dips his finger into the pot. Would you be willing to do what he asks?"

I could have sworn I saw just a hint of a smile at the corner of my father's mouth.

"What? How dare you ask such a thing of me?" Grandpa

went on like that for a while, but pretty soon he saw that my father was serious. As angry as he was, he couldn't bring himself to put his finger in boiling oil any more than I could.

Eventually he backed down, grabbed his dead bird, and stormed out of our house just as angrily as he'd come in.

I heard he and his sons ate that bird for dinner that night.

Grandpa had tried to force me into making a false confession, but I'd turned the pressure right back around on him. Though I wouldn't play poker for another thirty years, this was my first "all in" experience. I felt the pressure, and I might have buckled and confessed if they'd actually brought in the pot of oil, but I wasn't going to allow anyone to force me to do something I knew I shouldn't. I was innocent. More than that, I had to regain my father's trust at any cost. I went all in, and Grandpa never called.

Later that evening, after everyone had left our house, my father patted my head. "You did very well, Xao." It was his way of telling me he was proud of me. You must understand, Hmong fathers don't say such things to their sons. In our culture, male children are expected to act like men from birth. No father ever praises his son for doing what men are supposed to do. It's not that they don't love their sons, but they don't express such feelings openly. My father actually praised me, telling me I was not merely expected to be a man; I was one.

To survive in my world, I had to be.

3

"I Can Do This"

For the first thirty-plus years of my life, I never played a hand of cards. Growing up, I didn't play hearts or spades or go fish or even slapjack. Cards were strictly taboo in the Yang house. Not only had I never played cards, but I'd never played chess or checkers or backgammon or any other game that might become a gateway to gambling. My father didn't allow it.

"For five generations, we Yangs have known gambling is for fools," he'd say. "No one ever gambled their way into riches."

That's not to say I didn't bend my father's rules a time or two. When I was a boy in Laos, I would hustle my friends out of their marbles, which were carved by scratching small river rocks against big rocks.

The first time we did this, my buddies asked me how many they should make.

"Only two."

"Why?"

"More than two is bad luck. Don't you know anything? That's why God gave you only two nuts."

Since most Hmong are very superstitious, my buddies believed me. I knew they would. That's why when they weren't around, I went to the river by myself and made as many marbles as I could carry.

Our homemade marbles never lasted long. When my buddies' marbles broke in half, I'd pull some out from my stash. "I have a few extra that I collected from the last time we played. Tell you what. I'll give you two new ones in exchange for you doing my chores today."

My buddies had no choice but to make the trade. They could never hike all the way to the river, scratch out new marbles, and make it back to play before the sun set. No one ever caught on to the fact that I had rigged the game against them. I preferred to think of it as doing good business. I certainly didn't think of it as gambling. With twenty extra marbles hidden away, my game was anything but a gamble.

My hustling days would end when my family left for America. My father's rules would not. If you were a Yang, you did not play cards or any game that might ultimately lead to gambling. End of discussion.

Even after I grew up and moved out on my own, I never took up cards. To be honest, I never gave them a thought.

One Saturday night in 2005, my wife and I collapsed on the sofa in front of the television. If this had been a normal Saturday night, Sue would've been at work in one of the local casinos and I would've been in the back bedroom reading a book after finally getting our six kids off to bed.

But this particular Saturday came at the end of a tiring weekend. Some cousins from the Fresno area had come on Friday to spend the weekend with us in Temecula. My wife and I had taken time off work to spend the days with them.

Everyone who lives in Southern California gets to play tour guide for family who come to visit from outside the area. Like traffic and earthquakes, it's simply part of Southern California life. We'd been running around Coronado Beach and the rest of the region, and we were exhausted.

My cousins planned to leave the next morning and had headed off to bed early. Our six children were worn out, and they, too, had gone to bed without so much as a peep. That meant Sue and I finally had some time alone, just the two of us. For parents of young children, such moments are rare indeed. For parents of six children, they're next to nonexistent.

It was much too late to think about going out to a movie or restaurant, so Sue and I cuddled up on the sofa. I picked up the remote and flipped through channels, looking for something we could watch together before going to bed.

"What do you want to watch, Mommy?" In Hmong culture, couples with children usually call one another Mommy and Daddy.

"I don't care. Let's see what's on."

"Okay," I said and kept flipping through channels. "Hmmm, this looks interesting." I'd come to channel 144, ESPN.

"No, Daddy, keep going."

"I will, I will," I said, but I never did.

Sue let out a sigh.

I, on the other hand, was in the process of getting hooked. I'd never played poker or watched anyone play until tonight, when I came upon ESPN's broadcast of the World Series of Poker final table on this Saturday night in the fall of 2005.

The longer I watched, the more fascinated I became. I could tell right away the real game was only partially about the cards being dealt. I enjoyed the way players applied pressure by placing their bets in certain ways. While there's a lot of luck involved in the turning of the cards, these successful players weren't just lucky. They had to think, to study their opponents as well as the cards.

In Texas Hold 'Em, I saw a game, a sport, that seemed tailor-made for me. And for someone who doesn't enjoy many sports and is 5 feet 2, my options were limited.

"Daddy." Sue snapped me back into the moment of our quiet evening together. "Let's see what else is on."

If Sue had grabbed the remote, the television would already have been on HGTV. Any other night I probably would have switched to it for her. However, the thought of watching a couple from Long Beach try to choose between three houses was not nearly as appealing to me as the action unfolding at the final table of the previous year's World Series of Poker.

"Just a couple more minutes, Mommy. I promise. This is so interesting."

"I'm glad it is to you. Can I have the remote?"

We carried on variations of this conversation for nearly an hour.

Finally I stood, remote in one hand, pointing at the television with the other. "I can do this, Mommy. I can do this. And when I win, I will use the money for good."

My wife didn't say a word. She didn't have to. After my grand announcement, Sue gave me the look husbands dread, that look of disappointment and disapproval that said to me, *Jerry, don't even* think *of going there.*

I hate to say what I did next. You will probably think I'm the worst husband in the world. When I saw that look on my wife's face, I started giggling. I couldn't help myself.

Oh my. So much for our quiet time of cuddling on the sofa.

Sue shook her head and rolled her eyes. She wasn't amused, and she meant business.

Here I was, announcing I was not only going to take up poker but planned to win its biggest tournament in the world.

Sue didn't have to say anything. After eleven years of marriage, I knew exactly what she was thinking: *Jerry, we have six kids, a mortgage, and a car payment. How can you even think about throwing away our hard-earned money like this?*

I stopped giggling and sat next to her, closed my mouth, and didn't say another word. However, I did leave the television on channel 144.

My wife sighed. "How much longer do you plan on watching this?"

I pressed the guide button. "It's over at eleven, so just a little while longer. I really want to see who wins."

Another sigh. About fifteen minutes later, Sue stood up, stretched, and said, "I'm tired. I'm going to bed. Are you coming?"

"I'll be right behind you as soon as this is over."

"I'll probably be asleep when you come to bed." She gave me a quick kiss and walked toward our bedroom.

I didn't mention poker to my wife again for a few weeks, until she brought it up.

"What's that thick book you're reading?" she said to me one night.

I was sitting at a small desk in our bedroom, where I often did late-night reading for work. "This?"

"Yes. That doesn't look like one of your normal books."

"It's, uh, it's called *Super System* by Doyle Brunson."

"*Super System*? What kind of book is that?"

I sort of cleared my throat, swallowed hard, then said, "It's a, uh, a poker book." In fact, this book is considered *the* book on how to play poker. I've heard all the pros got mad at Brunson back when he wrote it in the 1970s because he gave away so many of their secrets.

"Daddy," Sue said, "you know how much I hate gambling. Almost every night at the casino, people play at my blackjack table and lose their grocery money for the following week. Or worse. And I see what that does to them while I deal the cards. They don't want to go home after they lose; they don't want to have to explain to their spouses why they won't be able to pay any of their bills for a long time. I cannot bear the thought of you going down that same road."

"Mommy, believe me, I would never do anything like that. I don't plan on becoming a gambler. Right now, I find the game of poker interesting, and I want to learn more about it. That's all."

"Okay," she said, but I could still see the fear in her eyes.

I didn't press the issue, but I had been serious when I'd made my announcement that Saturday night. I also knew I had a lot to learn. On the nights when my wife worked, and after all our children were in bed, I flipped through the satellite channels until I found poker. Instead of watching like a fan, I took notes. I also paid attention to the announcers' comments, especially Mike Sexton's and Vince Van Patten's from the World Poker Tour.

And I read books about poker. In addition to Doyle Brunson's book, I read Phil Hellmuth's *Play Poker Like the Pros*, which I'd heard was also required reading for anyone serious about poker. It was as if I'd gone back to school except now, instead of my college and grad school biology and psychology classes, my subject was poker.

The more I read and watched, the more convinced I became that this was the sport for me. However, I never betrayed my wife's trust in me. My involvement in poker would not go beyond reading books and watching televised matches if my wife remained opposed to the idea of my playing in a tournament or cash game.

After a month and a half of studying the game, I presented my plan. "Mommy, you know I'm disciplined with money. You know I never take funds we need as a family and waste them. We both work too hard for that."

She agreed.

"So here's what I want to do. I would like to try my hand at poker. I really think I can be successful at this game. I want to take 5 percent of my take-home pay each week, just $50, and use that to enter some tournaments. I promise you, I won't spend more than this. In fact, that is the only money I'll take with me into the card room when I play."

My wife knew I was telling the truth. "Okay, Daddy, you can do this. I'm behind you. You've been successful at everything else you've done. I know you can do this as well."

This was a special moment for me. Her trust meant everything to me. Now I just needed to get in the game.

4

Vegas or Bust

When I won the World Series of Poker in 2007, I stunned everyone in the Amazon Room of the Rio All-Suite Hotel & Casino, along with ESPN's announcers and the experts at the poker magazines. Yet probably no one was more surprised than the poker players who competed against me in my very first tournament in the fall of 2005. I spent most of that day completely lost, making one rookie mistake after another.

At one point, one of the players at my table turned to me and said, "This isn't a kiddy game, you know, buddy. Maybe you should go home and learn how to play before you enter a tournament."

I have to admit, this gentleman was right. I probably should have gone home and studied a little more before I tried playing in a tournament, even one with a $25 entry fee, or buy-in. Though I'd read several books about poker and watched hours of tournaments on television, I'd paid so much attention to strategy that

I'd failed to pick up some of the basics of the game, especially the terminology.

On my very first hand, I was in the third position at the table, which meant I was the first person to act. The small blind and big blinds were on the table.[4] I had to decide whether to (a) raise, which meant bet more than the big blind, (b) call, which meant place a bet equal to the big blind, or (c) fold, which meant throw my cards away and not play this hand. Those were my only options.

In this moment on my first hand, instead, I said, "I check," which meant I wanted to keep playing in the hand without making any kind of bet at all.

"I'm sorry, sir," the dealer said, "you must either raise, call, or fold."

Now here's where this story gets really embarrassing. I didn't know what it meant to call.

"Okay, I raise." It was the only term I knew.

"How much?"

"Uh, twenty."

Everyone at the table groaned.

"The minimum raise is twice the big blind," the dealer said.

"Oh, I'm sorry. Please be patient with me. I'm a rookie."

"I can tell," one of the other players said, laughing.

I didn't respond. For the rest of the tournament, I paid close attention to the terms and phrases the other players used. Only when I heard an opponent say "call" and then put in the same number of chips I'd just bet did I figure out what that term meant.

Not knowing the right words to use was the least of my

---

4. Blinds are mandatory bets placed into the pot before the cards are dealt. In Texas Hold 'Em, one player must bet the large blind, and the player immediately to his right must bet the small blind, which is half the size of the large blind. These increase in size as players move up levels of play. Each becomes part of that player's bet should he decide to stay in the hand. Responsibility for placing the blinds moves around the table on each hand.

problems that day. In No Limit Texas Hold 'Em, each player is dealt two cards and places bets based on those cards. After the first round of bets, the dealer burns one card, which means he sets it aside and it's not used in the hand; then he lays three cards faceup. Every player's hand is based on two hole cards combined with the three flop cards on the table. Players then bet on the flop. The dealer burns another card and deals one, called the turn card. Then come another round of bets, another burned card, and the final community card, also known as the river. A player's hand is based on the five best cards he can make with his two hole cards and the five cards on the table.

In an early hand in my first tournament, I had jack-eight of clubs as my hole cards. That's not very good. Today I'd almost always fold these cards, but in my first few tourneys I did what most amateurs do and played almost every hand. An eight turned up on the flop, which meant I had a pair of eights. The other two cards were both clubs. The turn card was something like the nine of diamonds, and the river was another club. When those still in the hand turned their cards, someone had a pair of queens. Thinking I'd lost, I turned my cards in disgust.

A woman next to me said, "Hey, buddy. You hit the flush. You won."

"I did?" I was completely shocked.

Several of the players at the table muttered things that I could tell weren't compliments.

I embarrassed myself further a little later in the round when someone announced they were going all in.

"What exactly does that mean?"

The rest of the players laughed.

Later I threw away my hand after the river card, which was the same as folding. Only then did I look closer and realize I'd actually won. Unfortunately, by throwing down my cards I'd given up the hand and the pot.

By the end of the day, many of the players were getting irritated with me, not merely because I kept making silly mistakes but because the cards always seemed to fall my way. Some days are like that, even for rookies who shouldn't last past the third or fourth hand. The other players at the table couldn't believe it when I kept winning pots and ended up finishing in the money, which means earning part of the prize because I came close enough to winning the tourney.

I walked out with $282.

After driving home from the tournament, I burst through the front door and announced to the family, "We're going to Chuck E. Cheese's tonight."

My kids were as happy as could be, but my wife wasn't quite as enthusiastic. She gave me one of those looks that said, *Yeah, yeah, yeah, that's great. Now quit while you're ahead.*

She still went with us to Chuck E. Cheese's.

Even as I celebrated with my family, I knew I'd been very lucky. On any given day, Texas Hold 'Em can be 90 percent skill or 90 percent luck. That day, it had been the latter.

The more important thing was that actually playing in a tournament had helped me understand how much more I had to learn. Again, I had one goal when I took up poker, and that wasn't to finish in the money at a local $25 buy-in Saturday poker tournament. No, I wanted to play in the main event of the World Series of Poker with its $10,000 buy-in. I knew I had a long way to go.

Once the last piece of pizza had been eaten and the euphoria of cashing out wore off, I dove back into my poker education process.

In my first tournament, not being able to speak the language of poker had labeled me immediately as a rookie and prime target for experienced players to pick off, to say nothing of how my playing itself had been an embarrassment time and again. I didn't want to make that mistake again.

I turned to Phil Hellmuth's *Texas Hold 'Em*, which I read from cover to cover, focusing especially on the twenty-plus-page "Phil's Glossary," which explains every poker term. Hellmuth also gave me insight into the personality of the players in any given poker room. Now he was speaking my language. The ability to read other players, to understand why they approach each hand the way they do, gives you a huge advantage at the table. Reading the other players goes beyond picking up on their tells, which are the telltale signs of whether they're bluffing or holding an unbelievable hand.

Today when I play, I spend the first thirty minutes to an hour just trying to figure out the personalities of the other players at the table. Most fall into three categories: passive, aggressive, and passive-aggressive.

The first are passive players. They play tight, which means they fold nearly every hand and play strictly when they have a pocket pair or two very high cards. Passive players focus solely on their cards and hardly pay any attention to the other players.

Aggressive players are the exact opposite. They play almost every hand and rarely fold. It doesn't matter what their hole cards might be. Whether they hold pocket aces or two-three off suit, they're in. Rather than focus on their cards, they try to play the other players. An aggressive player will bully others into folding out of fear that he's holding the nuts, that is, the best hand possible based on the cards on the table. From time to time, but not often, a very good player will be an aggressive player. Usually, aggressive players are beginners who still haven't learned the game. Even amateurs get lucky from time to time, though, which makes them dangerous at the table.

However, the most dangerous players of all are what I call passive-aggressive. These are the good players who know when to push and when to let up. As I said, the aggressive players are usually beginners; the passive players are often those who have been playing long enough to know that reckless play will get them beat but haven't yet perfected the art of reading other players. Passive-aggressive players are the ones who know what they're doing, the ones I want to learn from.

Knowing how each player approaches the game enables me to employ different strategies against each. This is a skill I'm still trying to master.

Looking back at my first try at poker, I realize I was the crazy, unpredictable player who played way too many hands. I know from personal experience that those players may get lucky from time to time, but they don't have the skills for continued success.

Most rookies and amateurs rely on nothing but luck. They look at their eight-two same suit and immediately think they can hit a flush, so they push all in, convinced Lady Luck is on their side. Sometimes they hit the flush, or they get really lucky and a couple of eights and a two turn up for a full house. Long-term, that's the worst thing that can happen. Hitting a lucky hand or two makes them even more reckless. In the end, they almost always end up busting out. Still they keep coming back for more, especially in tournaments and cash games with very low buy-ins.

My approach to the game changed when I decided to treat whatever money I risked as the last money I had on earth. If the tournament had a $25 buy-in, that became my last $25.

Most of my life, I was extremely poor. I knew how hard money was to come by. Even though I had a good job as a psychologist when I started playing poker, trying to raise a family in Southern California was expensive. We Yangs do not throw money away.

I tried to always keep this same mind-set in tournaments. I never carried more cash into the card room than I needed for the entry fee. And I always left my credit and debit cards at home so I wouldn't be tempted to go beyond what I needed for the tournament.

Playing as if the money I risked was all I had in the world provided the discipline I needed to settle down at the poker table. It also gave me a huge advantage over players with the attitude that "it's no big deal; it's only twenty-five bucks."

If I know I have another couple hundred dollars in my

pocket I can use to buy more chips or enter another game if I go bust, I'm far more likely to call or raise on a hand I should fold. The fewer marginal hands I play, the more likely I am to survive long enough to make the final table or at least finish in the money without having to hit a miraculous river card.

These were all lessons I was starting to learn.

In addition to reading more poker books, I watched more and more poker on television and recorded tourneys so I could really study the action. For me, poker on television was not entertainment but poker boot camp. Not only did I watch the way competitors played their hands, but I also paid close attention and took copious notes on the way they carried themselves at the table. I decided if I wanted people to respect me as a player, I should act like a serious player.

There was one problem: I didn't know what serious poker players acted like.

As I've mentioned, I look like anything but a card player. I knew if I dressed the way I normally did for work, everyone at the poker table would automatically count my chips as their own.

Watching on television, I noticed most of the top players dressed in all black, so I decided to dress in black when I played. Many of them also wore dark glasses, which I thought looked cool. If it was good enough for the pros, it was good enough for me. I topped off the look with a ball cap pulled low because that's how my favorite players on television wore theirs.

Chris "Jesus" Ferguson, whose nickname is inspired by his long hair and beard, was one of those favorites. He really does look like Jesus—if Jesus wore all black and a cowboy hat. Of course, he can pull off the look since he isn't a 5 foot 2 Hmong man.

Looks aside, I learned a lot from watching Chris Ferguson, especially the way he carries himself at the table. He always takes the same amount of time to make a bet, and he never gives off any tells. He almost looks like a statue at the poker table.

I, on the other hand, gave off one clue after another in those early days. I put my hand to my mouth when making a bet, which is a sure sign that someone's bluffing.

Watching pros like Chris Ferguson and another of my favorites, John Juanda, on television, I took note of where they put their hands when they bet, how they handled their chips, and even what they did after folding a hand. If you want to play like the best, you should learn from the best.

I knew, though, that books and televised events could only take me so far. Perhaps the most valuable thing I ever did to improve as a poker player was to humbly ask for advice from players I respected.

Back when I first started playing, several times I came up against a player named Charlie, who had been playing poker a long time. Whenever we faced one another, especially in head-to-head showdowns, it was almost as though he saw my cards before I did.

After one tournament, I spoke to Charlie. "I don't want you to give away all of your secrets, but I'm fascinated by the way you can read other players. Do you mind if I ask you questions from time to time about how I can improve my game?" Thankfully, Charlie agreed, and over the next couple of years, we exchanged e-mails and phone calls.

In addition to Charlie, I asked a few others how they

played certain hands. I noticed some taking notes at the table, so I asked them what exactly they were doing. They told me they noted how important hands played out and what they, along with others at the table, had done.

At the next tournament, I broke out my own notebook. Afterward, I reviewed how I'd played and what I'd done in certain situations.

Then I called Charlie. More than once, I asked, "What should I have done here?"

I also learned to watch people. All of the top poker books say you should never look at your cards as soon as they're dealt. Instead, you should look around the table and watch how your opponents react to their cards. Once your turn comes, then and only then you look. The same is true when the flop comes. Rather than watch the cards, watch other people's reactions to the cards. Good players sit as still as statues, but rookies and amateurs give off signs. They can't help themselves.

Watching other people helped me see some of the mistakes I kept making. By putting my errors next to theirs, I learned how to become a better player.

Too many beginners think poker is all about playing your cards. It isn't. Good players play their opponents. Of course, everyone gets burned by a lucky draw from time to time. The fact that I cashed in on my first tournament demonstrates that. But as I said, I knew luck couldn't carry me where I wanted to go as a player.

Since I played the local cash games and tournaments, I ended up going against some of the same players frequently. All the regulars knew I was a rookie, and more than one of them planned to take advantage of that.

Right before one of my first tournaments, I was standing in line, waiting to be seated, and one man said, "I have you figured out, Jerry Yang. I know your tells. I hope you brought a lot of money today because I'm going to take it all."

I smiled and didn't say a word. I knew right off he was trying to put me on tilt, which means playing with a chip on my shoulder or with emotion rather than discipline. A lot of players use this as part of their strategy. Not long after I won the World Series of Poker, one of the top pros tried to get me to play in a cash game with the same kind of taunt. Poker players who compete with emotion soon find themselves with an empty stack.

As luck would have it, this player and I ended up at the same table. He kept right on talking. "I know what you've got in your hand."

I refused to take the bait.

After a while, he stopped taunting and started muttering. "I don't know how you do it, you lucky b—." By the end of the round, he was just flat-out mad. He hadn't taken my money; I'd taken his.

Because we played in a lot of the same local tournaments, this happened more than once. The guy became very frustrated. He was a good player, yet for some reason every time I went up against him, the cards fell my way.

Finally, after I took all his chips once again, he looked at me and said, "You're like my f—ing shadow that follows me everywhere I go."

"Oh, come on," I said as politely as I could, "there's no need for profanity."

"I mean it; you are my f—ing shadow." He shot me the most hateful look.

Afterward, I thought a lot about what this guy had said. *The Shadow.* I believe in turning negatives into positives. The more I thought, the more I liked that label. So much, in fact, that it became my nickname, my poker persona.

Outside of the card room I was Jerry Yang, the mild-mannered psychologist who worked with foster families and at-risk children. But once I put on my black and my dark glasses and pulled my ball cap low, I became The Shadow.

It took a while, but I had finally become a real poker player, at least in my own mind. By my fourth tournament, the locals I played believed it as well. I not only cashed in; I actually won.

Instead of $282, this time I collected $4,000. I was so excited I tipped the dealer $400, more than twice as much as most people tip after a win. I didn't care. I wanted to share my happiness with everyone.

That night, my family and I once again had a great time at Chuck E. Cheese's.

I then put half of my winnings in the family savings account and the other half in my poker bankroll. The next week, I was back at the table, playing my last $25 in the world.

It wouldn't happen overnight, but I knew this path would eventually take me to my ultimate goal: Las Vegas.

5

A Not-So-Distant Thunder

No one else went to the farm with my father on this particular day. Only me. The two of us left our house at first light and hiked two hours through the jungle to the patch of ground he'd cleared for our next crop.

"We have a lot of work to do, Xao," he told me as we walked the winding trail descending to our farm. "You need to make sure you pick up every last twig, no matter how small, and put it into the brush pile. Do you understand?"

Even though I was seven, I was expected to work like a man. "Yes, Father." I struggled to match his pace on the trail, the small basket bouncing on my back.

"The field must be perfectly clear so we can plant next week."

I didn't realize it at the time, but I am now sure my father knew we would never plant anything in our field. Ever.

The distant sound of cannons and gunfire boomed closer. May was the month for planting in Laos, but May of 1975 was a bad month to be a soldier in General Vang Pao's army.

"You can count on me, Father. I'll make sure this is your cleanest field ever."

My father laughed. "I'm sure you will, Xao. I'm sure you will."

When we reached the field, I set right to work.

My father had already cleared the trees in the field but decided he needed to take out one or two more at the edges. "The shade will keep the rice plants on this side from growing as they should," he explained, just as his father had taught him, and as I would one day teach my son. It was the Hmong way. At least, it always had been.

My father grabbed his ax and chopped down the first tree. After it fell, he hacked it into pieces small enough to drag to the brush pile in the middle of the field. I scrambled around him, gathering every falling branch. Then we moved on to the next tree and the next, my father chopping while I worked hard to keep up with him.

After about three hours of work, something in the distance caught my father's attention. He dropped his ax and walked toward me, never looking away from whatever had caught his eye.

I didn't pay too much attention to what he was doing. Since we were hunters as well as farmers, I thought my father probably saw a deer or some other animal he might kill for our dinner. When I bent to scoop up another pile of branches, I felt a hand on my shoulder.

"Leave the sticks, Xao, and come with me." My father's

tone and expression sent a chill down my spine.

He grabbed my hand, and the two of us moved quickly toward the lean-to he'd built a few weeks earlier on the far end of the field. On a normal workday, the palm roof and open sides provided a shady place for a short break. Up ahead, I saw my uncle walking quickly down the hill toward our field.

I knew something bad must have happened because no one made the two-hour hike from our village to our farm for a purely social visit. "What's wrong, Father?"

"I don't know yet, Xao."

In retrospect, I believe he knew exactly. Whatever had happened, he'd been expecting it, even though he didn't want to admit it to himself.

My uncle arrived at the lean-to at the same time we did. Before he said a word, I knew something very bad had happened. I'd seen that expression many times. The heaviness on his face told me someone must have died. My grandmother still looked that way when she talked about my mother, who'd died when I was three.

"They've attacked Hin Haw,"[5] my uncle said.

I didn't have to ask who "they" were.

My father sighed. "Okay, go back home and do what you need to. Xao and I have to grab some food for the pigs, and then we'll be right behind you."

I turned to the field.

"Don't worry about the tools, Xao. Leave them. Get your basket. We need to leave right away."

We made a brief stop at a small stream, and I filled my

5. Names of villages and other places within this book are the Hmong names our family used.

basket with *qos dlej*, a large, leafy plant with a slimy, sticky sap, for our pigs. That was the one part of the hike back home that felt routine.

As the chief elder of our village, my father ordered everyone to come to our house that night.

By American standards, the house was not much with its bamboo walls and thatched roof, but in my eyes, it was a mansion. It was the biggest home in the entire village and the only one with running water. Using bamboo pipes, my father had engineered an aqueduct from a nearby stream straight to our front door. Everyone in the village came to our house to get water or do wash. My friends took their showers under our bamboo spigot. I thought my father was a genius.

On this night, though, no one cared about our running water or the size of our house. Nor had anyone taken time to cook dinner or do any of their usual evening chores. As soon as my father and I arrived in the village, word spread and the people dropped everything and headed our way. Those who couldn't get inside our house listened through the cracks in the bamboo walls.

I moved close to my father as he took his place at the front of the crowd, but I didn't come close enough to get in his way. Hmong families take seriously the old adage that children are to be seen but not heard, especially on a night like this.

"Let us pray." These were my father's first words that night.

I know even atheists have been known to say a prayer or two when things get bad enough, but my father didn't pray like someone with nowhere else to turn. He prayed with the confidence that God was still in control.

By the time my father said "amen," the dread that had permeated the room didn't feel quite so powerful, at least not to me. Strength and confidence came over me. I still felt fear, but it was no longer paralyzing.

"By now everyone knows what has happened in Hin Haw," my father said. "The Pathet Lao and the NVA attacked there, and it's just a matter of time before they arrive."

Some of the men gasped. A few women sobbed softly.

"The way I see it, we have two options, and fighting is not one. I fought these soldiers for many years, as did most of the men in this room. We can't defeat the Communists. Not now."

Around the room, men agreed.

"So here are our options. First, we can stay here and pray that when the Communist forces arrive, they do us no harm; we can try to reason with them and convince them this is our home and all we want is to work our farms and live in peace. Or we can escape to Thailand."

The cries in the room grew louder, but my father continued, unfazed. "So which of these two options should we choose? If these were reasonable men, we could try the first. If they were simply taking over the country and putting their people in complete control, they might listen to us. Yet that is not how the Pathet Lao or the NVA operate. They already have control of Laos. We pose no strategic threat to them. No, these soldiers attack the Hmong for one reason only: revenge."

Most of the men nodded.

"I and every man in this room who served under Vang Pao have seen the Pathet Lao's tactics firsthand. When they invade a village, they rape the women and girls. These so-called soldiers don't care how young the girls are. Rape is purely a means of torture for them. I have also seen with my own eyes what they did to the children of the villages they attacked. And the men . . ."

My father took a deep breath. "Let me simply say that anyone who resists them will soon wish they had not. My platoon came across the pits into which they had thrown both men and women after beating and torturing them. The Communist soldiers had used those pits as a latrine, urinating and defecating on those below. Most were left to starve to death. The lucky ones were shot and put out of their misery. These are not wild rumors or propaganda. I know these things to be true because I have witnessed the aftermath with my own eyes."[6]

I glanced around the room and found my buddies sitting close to their parents. The day before, all they'd cared about was getting out of their chores so they could go to the stream and play. Now horror covered their faces. I could only imagine how I looked.

"Even those who manage to stay alive are not safe," my father said. "In the eyes of the Pathet Lao, anyone who opposes them must be reeducated to see the wonders of Communism and the Pathet Lao. Entire villages have been sent to these re-education camps. Family units don't matter. Men are sent to one camp, women to another, children to another. The children are taught to hate their parents for opposing the Pathet Lao. Conditions in all the camps are horrendous, nothing more than another means of torture, another place for the Hmong to die." My father paused to let the weight of his words sink in.

6. Numerous human rights groups support these claims. To learn more, visit *Hmong International Human Rights Watch*, www.hmongihrw.org.

Some of the men knew my father's own brother had been captured and forced into the camps. I could hear murmuring across the room, along with continued crying.

My father remained in control of his emotions. "The Americans are gone and not coming back, and General Vang's army is no more. No one will rescue us. I believe we have no choice but to gather whatever we can carry and go as fast as possible to the Mekong River and Thailand. The Thai are the only friends we have left. We will be safe with them."

With that, my father stepped back to allow the rest of the village to respond.

Several women began making the Hmong cry of death. I cannot describe the horror that bloodcurdling wail brings. Every part of your body begins to melt away. It leaves you broken emotionally, spiritually, even physically.

Their husbands tried to stop them. "No, no, don't make that cry. Why are you doing that? We don't know what's going to happen, but if you keep making that cry, we all *will* die. Stop it right now."

My people are superstitious and believe reacting to such news with the cry of death seals your fate, allowing the evil spirits to swoop down and control you.

No matter how much the men protested, the cry rose and filled everyone with dread.

"How long will it take us to get to the Mekong?" a man asked.

"At least a week, maybe longer," my father replied. "We won't be able to travel on the main roads. We would surely be caught. I've scouted some trails through the jungle that I think we can use without being seen."

"What about my child?" one woman said. "He's just a baby. He can barely walk. How is he supposed to hike through the jungle for a week? He'll never survive."

Other women shouted out, and the cry grew even louder.

"We all have children," my father said. In fact, in our village, children outnumbered adults four to one. "We will simply do whatever we must to get everyone to safety, no matter how young or old. Please listen to me. We have no time to waste. The soldiers will arrive any moment. We must leave now."

The discussion went on for a long time, critics attacking my father's plan.

"We should just stay and take our chances," one woman yelled. "If we beg for mercy, surely they will spare us and our children."

One of the older men chimed in. "I think leaving is a very bad plan. How do you know our lives are in danger if we stay? You don't." Pointing at my father, he said, "You want us to leave everything behind all because of something you saw in the war, but the war is over. We aren't soldiers here. At least, most of us aren't. Perhaps your life is in danger because you fought against the Pathet Lao, but I have no grudge against them. Why should we leave to protect you?"

The man's son, an older man with a family of his own, joined in the attack.

My father didn't waver. "I'm not trying to frighten anyone into doing anything. These are the facts. You can go to other villages and witness the destruction for yourself. You can see the broken bodies of babies smashed on the rocks. You can talk to the survivors, the women brutally raped and then forced to watch as their husbands' and brothers' abdomens were slit open before they were left to die slowly. These are not wild stories anyone made up. These are the facts. We have no choice. If we're to live, we must escape."

The weeping and wailing grew louder, but my father didn't have to try to quiet them. The other men in the room, all of whom were related to our family, moved through the crowd and calmed everyone.

One man, who proved to be the most critical of my father, refused to settle. He kept contradicting and questioning him. Finally the man said, "All of you may leave, but my family is staying. This is our home, and we refuse to run away in fear."

"Very well," my father said. "You must do what you believe is best for your family."

This quieted the critics once and for all.

As soon as the man and his son left the meeting, the discussion turned from the question of whether we should escape to full-scale planning for the journey.

I walked toward my older brother across the room and sat next to him. "This is like Moses leading the people out of Egypt."

"Yeah, and Father is Moses," he said.

Any other time, I would have laughed. I couldn't then.

Like the night the Israelites decided to escape, this night for our family was different from any other.

Once everyone left our house that night, I talked to my father. "Are we going to leave in the morning?"

"No, Xao." He did his best not to show his exhaustion.

"We cannot risk having 100 people go walking along in broad daylight. The soldiers would catch us for sure. No, we will leave tomorrow evening, right after the sun sets. Now get to bed. Sleep. Tomorrow will be a busy day."

I lay down next to my brother on our bamboo bed. Neither of us could sleep. We talked through the night about the journey ahead of us, as well as what we would miss the most about our home. I didn't want to say it, but I kept thinking there was a good chance one or both of us might not survive.

I tried to chase the thoughts from my mind. I'd already lost my mother; I couldn't bear the thought of losing a brother. I finally drifted to sleep to the sound of neighbors asking my father for advice about what to take or how to prepare food for the journey.

I woke and rubbed my eyes. For a split second, all thoughts of soldiers and escapes through the jungle felt like nothing more than a hazy dream. The view from my bamboo bed was exactly as it had been every morning.

Reality fell on top of me when an artillery shell exploded somewhere in the distance.

What happened last night? It felt like I was experiencing the feelings from the night before for the first time: the fear, the pain, the sense that soldiers might appear in our village at any moment and we would all die.

The morning sun filled my room as a beautiful new day greeted me, but I knew appearances were deceiving. This morning was not the beginning but the end. On this day, life as I had always known it ceased to exist.

6

Escape

I walked outside and found my father. He was too busy slaughtering one of our pigs to notice me. Any other day, all the boys in the village would have been surrounding him, hoping to get the first chance at the pig's bladder. While that may sound disgusting to Western readers, to the kids in our village, getting a pig's bladder was like unwrapping a birthday present.

None of us had ever seen a real ball. Instead, whenever one of our fathers slaughtered a pig, we blew up the bladder and kicked it around until it popped. If we were lucky, we could kick one around for two days. On rare occasions, we could squeeze three days out of one but only if we stopped the game every few minutes to wet the skin to keep it from drying out.

"Good morning, Father," I said.

"Oh, good morning, Xao. Here. I have something for you." He handed the pig's bladder to me.

For a moment I forgot about the coming soldiers and

having to escape through the jungle as soon as the sun sank. "Thank you, Father." I grabbed the bladder and ran into our house to find a strip of cloth to tie off the end after blowing it up.

My buddies were all busy doing chores, and my father had sent my brother to the barn to feed the animals. With no one around to play, I practiced dribbling the makeshift ball on my knees. It was all so surreal, as if this were just another day in Laos. I could still hear the gunfire in the distance, but then again I'd heard it every day of my life. Today felt no different.

My mother and grandmother were busy cooking rice and frying up the pigs my father had butchered.

Though they cooked all day, we didn't eat much. All the food was for our trip. They stuffed the rice and pork into the hollow part of bamboo branches and sealed the tops of each, turning the bamboo into primitive thermoses. Every woman in the village was busy doing the same while the men butchered animals, gathered weapons, and prepared.

Every so often, someone from our village approached my father with questions about how much to pack or the best way to turn a bamboo branch into a food container. I will never forget one visitor.

My great-uncle, "Grandpa," the one who had wanted me to dip my finger in boiling oil, said in a hushed tone, "Youa, we need to talk. Privately."

They walked near our stable, where no one could hear them.

No one, that is, but me. I sneaked around behind them and found a place in the bushes where I could listen. I couldn't help myself. I was a very curious boy, which is a polite way of saying I was nosy.

"Youa, we have a problem." Grandpa's words struck me as funny in light of all the problems we faced in that moment.

"How so, Yang You Chong?"

"My son and his wife have just had a baby, and that baby cannot stay quiet." He might as well have been talking about our family. My youngest brother was barely a month old.

"Many families in the village have babies. What of it?"

"Long ago when our people left China, they had to escape through the night just like us. The Chinese almost caught them because of the crying of the children. Our ancestors found a way to keep the children quiet."

Grandpa didn't need to say anything more. Everyone in my village knew the story well. Parents had mixed opium with water and force-fed it to their children to sedate them.

Opium was common in the hills of Laos. My father had warned me how dangerous it was. I wanted to jump out from where I was hiding and scream, "No, Father, don't do it. Don't let them bring it. They'll try to give it to Boun My. I don't want him to die!"

But I didn't say anything. I simply crouched and listened.

My father looked at Grandpa for a long time. "Do you really believe this is necessary?"

My father knew Grandpa had more than one reason for bringing opium along. Many people in our village were addicted to it, and Grandpa was one of them. However, my father did not feel it was his place to question him. Hmong people respect the wisdom of their elders.

"Yes, very necessary."

"Very well. If you feel it's necessary, bring it along."

Again, I wanted to run to my father and beg him to forbid Grandpa from bringing this horrible stuff with us. But I didn't. I couldn't. Soon, I would wish I had.

The last day in our village flew by.

Just before sunset, my father went to our stable, opened the gate, and set our horses free. They took off running. I don't know where they went or what happened to them. We never saw them again.

He also opened the gate to the pigpen and tried to force the pigs out. They waddled out to pasture for a bit, then went right back to the small shed my father had built for them.

I guess they weren't afraid of the Pathet Lao and North Vietnamese soldiers. Not that I blame them. We treated our pigs well, but in the end we still butchered them. Their fate was the same no matter who fed them.

Rather than leave our valuables where the soldiers could carry them away, my father sealed them in a cave behind a waterfall at the nearby stream. Even though we didn't have much, our few treasures had been passed down from generation to generation. By hiding them in this cave, my father was, in effect, telling the villagers he expected to return someday.

Others followed his lead. By the end of the day, the vault was full. My father even placed his army M-16 there. He knew carrying such a weapon would immediately identify him as a former soldier in Vang Pao's army, a guaranteed death sentence.

As afternoon turned into evening, families began gathering in the main part of the village. No one had to announce it was time to leave. The sinking sun did that.

The older man and his son who had criticized my father so harshly in the meeting the night before didn't join us. Neither did their families. They stayed behind, just as they'd promised.

Once it was clear that everyone who planned to leave with us was ready, my father simply said, "Let's go," and we headed out. I carried on my back a large bag of rice, as heavy as I could manage. Since I only owned one pair of pants and one shirt, I didn't have to worry about luggage. I didn't have any shoes, either, but hardly anyone did.

The trail out of the village wound between my friends' houses. As we passed the empty homes, I thought about the good times we'd had there, but soon fear swept away those good thoughts. I wondered if any of us would make it through this alive.

We also walked past an empty house that the men of our village had built for the schoolteacher, Bee Vang. He'd come from far away and taught the children of our village to read and write, but when the war had drawn too near, he and his wife had gone back to their home village.

He'd said they would return when things got better. They never had.

On the very edge of the village sat one last building: my father's church. He'd served as the pastor for nearly a decade, ever since he'd completed his training with the American missionaries in Vientiane.

My father paused at the front of the church. "We are all leaving, and we will not come back," he said to the building. "It's okay. It is time to go."

Even though we are Christians, we are still Hmong, and Hmong tradition says that when you leave a place, part of your spirit stays behind. That's why my father said what he did. He was telling our spirits that we were leaving and calling them to come with us.

In that moment the finality of our departure hit me. I wanted to throw up.

Just past the church building, the trail into the jungle went up a hill. About halfway up, I turned and looked back at our village. I could still see smoke curling up from the houses into the sky as if the people who lived there were cooking their evening meals. Animals milled in pastures, and I expected to see children running by, laughing and kicking a pig bladder.

From up on the hill, everything looked completely normal, as if life had not changed one bit and never world. I have never forgotten that sight.

Looking back toward our village, I saw my father's favorite hunting dog, Lie, running up the trail after us. I loved that dog. He wasn't just a dog; he was part of our family. Every time my father went hunting, Lie was at his side. He'd chase the deer or whatever my father was after that day. No other dog in our village compared to him. In a sense, Lie put food on our table by leading the hunters to the prey. All of us, including my father, loved that dog.

When I saw him, I said, "No, Lie, you can't come with us."

My father heard me and turned around. "Go home, Lie," he shouted. "Go home."

Lie stopped, tail wagging.

"Go, I said!"

Lie turned around and walked maybe 100 yards toward home. Once my father's back was turned, though, he reversed direction.

"No," my father yelled with a hateful tone that said he meant business.

He wasn't being cruel. We didn't know if we had enough food for the people in our group, much less a dog. Besides, we couldn't take the risk; Lie's barking might give us away.

I watched as Lie turned and trotted back down the hill. It wasn't long before I saw him bounding up the trail once again. I guess he thought we were off on some great adventure, and he wanted to come along.

My father didn't yell this time. "Keep going. I'll catch up with you in a moment."

I can still see Lie standing there, that excitement on his face as if to say, *Let's go hunting!*

That was the last time I saw Lie.

My father stayed quiet for a long time after he rejoined our group. I couldn't bring myself to ask right then, but I knew what he had been forced to do.

Even now, after all these years, I miss that dog.

As we headed deeper into the jungle, we had to walk almost single file. I didn't remember the trails being so narrow on the hunting trips I'd taken with my father. Then again, we'd never taken the entire village with us before.

Two men led the way. One carried a torch made out of strips of bamboo tied together. The other used a machete to clear the undergrowth.

Night fell. I couldn't see anything except the fire far in front of my family. I stayed in line by holding on to my brother's shirt. He held on to my mother, who held on to the person in front of her, and so on, all the way up the line to the man with the torch. Children too small to walk rode on their mothers' backs in slings called *hlaab nyas*.

We'd walked a short distance into the dark when I stepped on a rock, cutting my foot. A short while later, I tripped over a stick that cut my other foot. More rocks. More sticks. Blood ran out of both my feet. We came upon a dead tree. I climbed up and over it. I didn't see the thorns lying on the other side until my feet landed on them. I struggled to pull out the thorns with one hand while holding on to my brother with the other.

Tree frogs' croaking echoed through the jungle, louder than I'd ever heard. Off in the distance, monkeys howled. Other animals chimed in. The darkness closed in around me. Fear crept down my spine, while pain radiated up from my feet and through my legs.

Suddenly, the blackness of the night turned neon green as a swarm of fireflies danced around me. The boy in me wanted to catch as many as I could, but I didn't dare let go of my brother's shirt or step out of line. I kept on marching.

We didn't stop to rest until about midnight.

My body wanted to sleep, but I didn't let myself doze off. Oh, my feet hurt so bad.

"What's the matter, Xao?" my mother said.

I showed her my bleeding feet.

She tore off strips from her dress and wrapped them. "This will make them feel better."

She was right. My feet felt a little better, until I started walking.

My father pulled my brother and me aside right before we took off again. "Xay, Xao, when I say it's time to get going, you must get right in line. Don't fall behind. It's too easy to get lost out here in the dark if you fall behind."

My father didn't have to tell me twice. My older brother and I made a pact. We would never leave camp without each other.

The first rest stop gave me a hint of what to expect during life on the run. My belly ached, and I could hear my brother's stomach rumbling. All of us were hungry. My father took one of the bamboo thermoses filled with rice, split off a small portion, and handed it to me.

"Thank you, Father." The portion of rice was a fraction of what I usually ate for a meal at home, but I didn't dare say a word.

My father had already made it clear that we had to make our food last for the entire journey, and no one knew how long that might be. "Drink lots of water," he said to my brother and me. "You'll need it to keep your strength up." Then he smiled and walked away.

Looking back, I realize he wanted us to drink enough to

make the hunger pains go away.

After a short rest, my father said, "Let's move on. We have a long way to go before the sun comes up."

We marched on through the night.

From time to time, I grabbed a handful of leaves whenever we passed a plant I knew to be edible. The people in front and behind did the same.

Up ahead, I heard a baby cry. And cry. And cry.

"Shut that kid up," a woman said.

The baby kept crying.

"You have to do something about that kid," another woman chimed in. Then another. And another.

The men didn't say anything. In Hmong culture, when women argue with one another, the men stand back and let them go at it.

"I'm trying to calm him," the child's mother said.

I felt sorry for her. I knew how much my baby brother cried on a normal night, and this night was anything but normal. Other babies had cried throughout the night's journey, but they'd all quieted quickly. Not this child.

"Stop trying and do something. You're going to get us all killed," a woman said so loudly that any Communist soldier within half a mile would've heard her.

"Give it some opium. That'll quiet it," someone else said.

"Yeah, opium. That's a great idea," another said.

The mother pled, "I can get him to settle down without opium. Just give me a minute."

"We don't have a minute. If you don't shut that kid up, I will," a woman said, and to me it sounded like a threat to do more than give the child opium.

Finally, my father had had enough. "Cut it out. If you women don't stop arguing, you and your families will have to go your own way. I will not hesitate to split us up just to get away from your constant bickering. You're worse than any crying child."

"But the baby won't stop."

"Give the mother time. She'll get it quiet. But I've had all of this arguing I can stand. It stops now."

The women fell silent for a time, but I feared the worst was yet to come.

Even though my father didn't approve, many of the parents used opium to keep their children quiet. Some of those children were never the same. Ever.

Neither were many of the adults from my village. The argument over the crying child frightened me, not because the baby might give away our position but because of what I saw in the people. I was aware that the stakes were life and death. I understood how we could be caught at any moment. Even so, I never expected to see these women, people my parents had taught me to respect, behave with such venom. Here we were, risking our lives to escape soldiers who wouldn't hesitate to kill us, and yet one crying child pushed some within our own group to the brink of committing murder.

I now understood that simply surviving the jungle would not be enough. Not if it meant sacrificing what should never be sacrificed.

7

Two Tournaments, One Prize

I had two options for getting into the World Series of Poker main event.

The first was to build up my bankroll over time until I had the $10,000 to buy a seat. Whenever I finished in the money in any tournament or cash game, I always put half the money in our family's savings account and the other half into my poker bankroll. My entry fee for my first few tournaments had come out of the 5 percent of my paycheck that I set aside each week. After about six months, I had enough in my bankroll for my poker hobby to support itself. My wife was very happy about that.

As my bankroll grew, I played in bigger tournaments with larger buy-ins and payouts. By the start of 2007, I'd built up more than $5,000, which meant, theoretically, I was halfway to a seat in the main event.

However, I would never in a million years spend $10,000 to enter a single tournament. I am a businessman, and from a business perspective, it makes no sense to risk $10,000 in a tournament with over 6,000 entrants from around the world. In a tournament where fewer than 10 percent cash out, you have to be very lucky to win no matter how good you may be. Even if I had $100,000 in my bankroll, I would never risk $10,000 on one tournament.

That left me with only one option in my quest to make it to the World Series of Poker main event: I had to play my way in.

I entered my first qualifying tournament on the last Saturday of January of 2007 at the Pechanga Resort & Casino. I knew the place well. I'd played my first tournament there. Since then, I had become a regular at its Saturday tournaments, especially those with low buy-ins. The World Series of Poker qualifier had a $225 buy-in, which was nine times the entry fee to my first tourney in 2005. In my first attempt to make it to the main event, I didn't do well.

In February, I went back to Pechanga and tried again. I fared a little better, making it all the way to the final table, but that was as far as I got.

In March, I finished second, which gave me hope for April.

Unfortunately, in April I busted out early.

That left May as my last chance to win a seat.

Saturday, May 26, 2007, Memorial Day weekend, was the last Saturday World Series of Poker qualifying tournament of the season. I left the house early to make sure I got a spot.

I decided not to drive the three or four blocks to the casino where I'd tried and lost four times already. To be completely honest, I'd spent so much there already trying to qualify that I didn't really want to have to lay down another $225.

Another nearby casino, Lake Elsinore Hotel & Casino, also featured a main event qualifying tournament with a buy-in of only $110. As I said, I'm a businessman. If I can save $100 and still win a seat to the World Series of Poker, I will make that deal every time.

At Lake Elsinore I'd played many Saturday tournaments and knew many of the players. This time I also saw a few new faces. Players came from all over Southern California with the same dream as mine: Vegas.

I knew this was my absolute last chance for the year to make it to the World Series of Poker, and I had to play my best. *Stay focused; be disciplined; do not lose your patience,* I kept telling myself. *Don't beat yourself! Wait for a good hand; then pounce.*

About half an hour into the first round, my first chance came. I drew pocket jacks. I made a modest raise before the flop, one just large enough to determine whether someone had a larger pair than mine. Anyone holding pocket kings or aces or even queens would have raised.

All but one player folded, and he merely called.

Very good. Slow play these jacks, and let the pot build.

The flop made my hand look even better. No queens. No kings. No aces. I don't remember all the cards, but I do remember that the dealer turned a nine. Even if someone paired the nine, I had this hand won.

In poker, the sooner you push other players out of a hand,

the better. If you have a chance to take a pot before the flop, you do it. More cards on the table represent more chances for someone to get lucky. I didn't want to take that chance.

The first to act, I said, "I'm all in."

The other player in the hand had a chip lead on me but not one so large that he would risk his tournament with nothing higher than a nine on the table. I knew he would fold.

"I call," he said.

The moment he turned his cards, I felt sick. He held pocket nines, with a nine on the board. Three nines always beat two jacks.

I had to get lucky on the turn or the river and draw to stay alive. The dealer didn't waste any time laying the turn and river on the table. The jack didn't come.

Not only had I not won a seat to the World Series of Poker, but I was one of the first players to bust out.

I stood, took off my glasses, and shook the player's hand. "Good luck to you, my friend." I said it with a smile, though inside I felt absolutely ill. I am not a patient man when it comes to meeting my goals. Baseball fans may say, "There's always next year," but I didn't want to wait another year. I walked outside, disappointed and more than a little mad at myself.

When I got to the car, I looked at my watch. That's when it hit me: *If I don't hit any traffic, I actually have time to get to Pechanga before their tournament starts.*

I normally don't play more than one event in a day.

I decided to make an exception.

Thankfully, traffic was light on Interstate 15 that Saturday morning. I exited onto Highway 79, which was also the exit for my home. As soon as I pulled off the freeway, I started having second thoughts. *Do I really want to risk another $225? I've already lost over $100 today. That's enough.*

Up ahead was the traffic light where I had to make the difficult decision. I could go straight through the light to get home. *But if I don't turn right on Pechanga Parkway,* I thought, *I'll have to wait a whole year for my shot at the main event.*

I turned right.

I made it to Pechanga with a few minutes to spare. Including me, 188 players entered. Of the $225 entry fee, $25 went to the casino and the rest went into the prize pool, giving us a total payout of over $37,000.

Since only those who make the final table cash out, making it there would make this a profitable day for those who wanted to merely finish in the money. I was not one of those people.

After falling flat earlier in the morning at Lake Elsinore, I played the first few hands at Pechanga tight. A tournament this size demands patience, not reckless aggression. Although I always play to win, I knew gaining the chip lead right out of the blocks wouldn't guarantee anything. In Texas Hold 'Em, you can go from the chip leader to busted flat in a matter of only one or two hands. I knew it from experience.

Play started at ten in the morning. By the afternoon, I found myself in the top 25 percent in terms of my chip stack.

Be patient. Do not overplay your hand. Let the cards come to you, I reminded myself.

Too many players who start off strong get themselves into trouble by letting their adrenaline get the best of them. They start playing marginal hands and soon find themselves in the short stack or worse. I fought the urge. I knew I didn't have to knock out all the other players myself. Sometimes the best play is to fold, sit back, and allow the other players to destroy one another.

My patience paid off. For the third time in five months, I made the final table. I was determined to force a different outcome.

When play began at the final table, I had the sixth or seventh largest stack, which is another way of saying I was in the bottom third. One player held what appeared to be an insurmountable lead. No sooner had the final nine taken our places at the table than one or two players brought up chopping the pot. That means they wanted to end the tournament immediately, divide the prize pool evenly among the nine of us, and let the chip leader have the seat at the main event.

I hated the idea. Luckily for me, I wasn't alone. The chip leader, a man named John, stopped the conversation dead in its tracks. "Let's just play and see what happens."

That was fine with me. I wanted to win, not settle for one-ninth of the prize money.

Two hours passed. The final nine were now pared down to four.

"Let's chop," a player said.

John still held the chip lead and shot the idea down once again. Since he'd maintained his lead throughout the final table, he didn't see any reason to lessen the pressure on the rest of us.

I now held the second largest stack and didn't want to chop the pot either.

Play continued for a long time. Finally, two other players busted out, leaving only me and John. He still held the chip lead, but I'd closed the gap considerably.

"I'll tell you what, Jerry," he said. "The casino gives a cash prize of $1,700 along with the seat at the main event. Here's what I'll do. You give me the seat, and I'll give you the extra cash. You put that with your second place money, and that's a pretty nice payday. Wadda ya say?"

"I appreciate the offer," I said, "but playing in the World Series of Poker is a dream of mine, too. Let's play the cards and see what happens."

"Suit yourself."

Head-to-head play is different from going up against nine or ten players. You must be cautious, but at the same time, you can't sit back and fold time and again. The blinds increase every few hands, which forces more and more of your chips into the pot. If you never take a chance and play a hand, the blinds alone will knock you out of the tournament.

John and I went back to the game for about an hour. I managed to grab a two-to-one chip lead, which meant now I could dictate the action. Yet I still had to be cautious. Leads have a way of disappearing fast in Texas Hold 'Em.

Sometime around four in the afternoon, the dealer gave me an ace-nine in the big blind. If not for my dark glasses, John would have seen my eyes open wider. I'd been waiting for a hand like this.

John acted first and raised.

"I re-raise," I said.

John thought for a moment, then said, "I'm all in."

Now it was my turn to act. With a sizable chip lead, I could afford to take a chance, even though losing would mean flipping from the chip lead to the short stack. I looked at my opponent, who fidgeted in his seat and rubbed his face with his left hand. I didn't know for sure that he was bluffing, but I decided to find out.

"I call," I said.

I could tell by the look on John's face that those were the last words he wanted to hear.

As soon as I turned my cards, he shook his head. He knew he was beat. "Good call, Jerry."

I looked at his cards. He had an ace, which meant he hadn't bluffed. But his other card was a lowly five.

I pumped my fist. "*Yes.*"

Another ace came up on the flop, which was good for me. However, a three or a four also came up, which meant John might possibly hit a straight. The turn card came: a jack.

He couldn't make his straight. Only a five on the river could beat me now. The dealer burned a card, then turned a seven.

I jumped and shouted, "Praise the Lord," at the top of my lungs.

I was on my way to Vegas.

The poker room manager shook my hand. "Congratulations,

Jerry. You played a great tournament."

"Thank you." It was all I could say. Honestly, I was in shock and couldn't believe I'd just won.

"Now, Jerry, the grand prize can be paid out in one of two ways. You can take the seat at the main event, or we will give you a check for $10,000. Which do you prefer?"

Oh my. Answering that question was my toughest call of the day. On the one hand, the main event had been my goal since the day I'd first discovered poker two years earlier. This was truly a once-in-a-lifetime opportunity. On the other hand, $10,000 is a lot of money. If Sue had been standing next to me, I knew she would've said, "Daddy, what are you waiting for? Take the money."

But my wife was not standing there with me, and I didn't call her to ask what she wanted me to do. For a moment, I wanted to say, "Write the check," but I didn't. "Playing in the World Series of Poker is my dream. I will take the seat at the tournament."

The manager smiled. "Well, it looks like your dream has come true. You are going to Vegas, Jerry."

I could hardly believe it. In six weeks, I, Jerry Yang, would take my seat in the biggest, most prestigious poker tournament in the world.

8

Between the Rio and the Roach Motel

When I won my seat at the main event of the World Series of Poker, I won just that: the seat. I didn't win an all-expense-paid trip to Las Vegas. The $1,700 cash prize that the Pechanga Resort & Casino gave me didn't come close to covering the cost of a hotel room and food for the twelve days of the main event. If I'd stopped and thought about it logically, I would've realized $1,700 was more than enough for an amateur player to drive to Vegas, see the sights, and then get knocked out on the first day of play. The thought never entered my mind.

The main event lasted twelve days, and that's how long I planned to stick around. I may have had a million-to-one shot to win it all, but in the back of my mind I kept thinking, *You never know. Stranger things have happened.*

I searched hotels online and made a few calls. The Rio All-Suite Hotel & Casino, site of the World Series of Poker, offered a special room rate for players, but even with their 50 percent discount, the $200 a night price tag was way out of my range. Other hotels in the area around the Rio were just as expensive.

"Wow," I said to my wife, "this is going to cost more than I thought."

That's when I had an idea. I'd go back to the Pechanga and ask the manager if the casino might help cover my hotel expenses. It seemed logical to me.

Not to him. "I'm sorry, Jerry, but that's not our policy." End of discussion.

In my lifetime, I've learned the value of persistence and having a backup plan. I drove back up Interstate 15 to the Lake Elsinore Hotel & Casino, where I'd busted out in half an hour trying to win their qualifying tournament. I hoped no one there remembered that little fact.

I found Pat Wilmes, the poker room manager. "I won a seat to this year's World Series of Poker at Pechanga," I said, "but they won't give me a hotel room in Vegas. You know how much I play here in your casino. Would you be willing to cover my hotel room for me?"

To my surprise, Pat said yes. "All we ask, Jerry, is that you wear a ball cap with our logo and one of our shirts."

"I'm happy to do that. Thank you very much." Wearing a hat in exchange for a hotel room sounded like a sweet deal to me.

"Do you care which hotel we put you in?"

I'd been to Las Vegas only one time, and that had been to make my marriage official.

Sue and I had been married in the traditional Hmong

way, with the elders coming to our home and us making our vows. Since the state of California doesn't recognize the traditional Hmong wedding ritual, though, we had also needed to get married someplace that would give us a state-approved license. Since it's cheaper to get married in Nevada than California, we went there. Even then, we didn't spend the night in Vegas. We basically rushed in, went through the ceremony, and drove home.

Judging by the little I'd seen in my brief time there, I decided one "hotel and casino" was just about like every other. "As long as I have a place to go to sleep, I'll be happy," I said.

Pat called me a couple of weeks later and gave me the name of my hotel and driving directions. "It's not on the Strip but downtown. Is that all right?"

"Sure," I said. On the Strip or downtown: how different could one be from the other? I was going to Las Vegas to play in the World Series of Poker. Nothing else really mattered.

The 6,000 players competing in the main event start their tournaments on one of four days, July 4, 5, 6, or 7. That is the only way to fit everyone into the Amazon Room. When I won my seat, I could choose any of the four days. I almost chose the third start date, July 6. I figured even if I busted out, I would have at least one extra day to hang out in Las Vegas and enjoy the sights and sounds of the World Series of Poker.

Right before I wrote July 6 on my form, though, I remembered a dream I'd had back in 2005. In my dream, I was riding in a helicopter with several of my friends. Thick fog covered the ground below. We had to get to the airport, but the pilot couldn't find it in the thick fog. Everyone in the helicopter in my dream panicked. Low on fuel, the plane was about to crash. The pilot radioed the control tower and cried out for help.

In my dream, I heard the voice of the air traffic controller. "Don't worry. I know exactly where you are. Descend slowly through the fog until you see the numbers on the runway. That's where you need to land."

The pilot in my dream did as he was instructed, and the gray fog obstructed my view through the window. Suddenly I saw the numbers on the runway, just as the air traffic controller had said. I never forgot that sight or the numbers: 7–7–7.

That dreamed flashed in my mind as I stared at my main event entry form. I knew when my tournament needed to begin: July 7, 2007.

Even though I chose the fourth and final day, I drove to Vegas a day early. I wanted to give myself plenty of time to walk around the Amazon Room and take in the World Series of Poker before I actually started play.

Before that, I wanted to check into my hotel. I took the downtown exit off Interstate 15 and turned right. I nearly made a U-turn. *This can't be right*, I said to myself when I pulled up in front of my hotel. It looked like a scene out of an old cop show. Trash covered the parking lot, and the asphalt was all broken up. A couple of drunks leaned against one of the dilapidated buildings neighboring the casino.

No, no, no, this can't be the place. How am I going to stay here . . . for twelve days?

I got out of my car, locked it, and walked toward the hotel lobby, leaving my luggage in the trunk. I thought, *If the inside is as bad as the outside, I have to find another place to stay. This won't work.*

When Pat from Lake Elsinore had told me the hotel was downtown rather than on the Strip, I hadn't realized the difference. And when he'd told me he was able to get the room for just under $700, I'd thought, *Wow, this must be a really nice hotel.* Clearly, $700 wasn't much in Vegas.

On my way to the lobby door, I stepped around a couple of prostitutes working the street in front of the hotel. Inside, stains spotted the carpet. The lobby itself was dark, even in the daytime. The fluorescent lights gave off a dingy, otherworldly glow. Off to the side of the check-in desk, repairmen worked on one of the two elevators, a large "Out of Order" sign hanging above them.

"What have I gotten myself into?" I said to no one in particular.

I walked to the check-in desk but paused before ringing the bell. Part of me wanted to turn around, walk away, jump in my car, and find another place, anyplace, besides this broken-down dump. But I didn't have a choice. I'd brought enough money to cover only my food.

I let out a long sigh. *Okay, Jerry, this place leaves a lot to be desired, but at least it's paid for.* I took another look around the lobby. *Besides, I've stayed in worse places. A lot worse.*

On my way up to my room, the one working elevator creaked and moaned like a rope about to break. I fully expected it to stop at any moment.

My mind jumped back to the nursing home in Fresno where I'd worked when I was in high school. Back then, I'd clocked in at three in the morning, worked for four hours, then headed off to school. One morning my mop bucket and I had gotten stuck in an elevator for two hours. The Otis Elevator guys had finally shown up and pried the door open, setting me free.

Back then, I'd only been late for class. Listening to the hotel elevator groan now, I wondered, *What if I get stuck in this thing and miss my start time? But what's my other option? Walking down a dark stairwell and getting mugged?*

I wished I'd been more specific about where I wanted to stay.

The second I opened my hotel room door, a stench hit me. The room smelled as if a chain smoker had left a pile of wet towels in one corner for a week or so. I flipped the light switch, but it didn't seem to make the room any brighter. The light fixture had turned yellow years before.

How will I ever get any sleep in this place? I can hardly breathe.

I went into the bathroom and turned on the light, which sent roaches scrambling for cover. Mildew crawled up the cracked shower tile. *Just great.*

I walked back into the room, sat on the bed, and grabbed the television remote. *Let's at least see what channels they have.* I began pushing buttons. Nothing happened. *That's it.*

I picked up the phone and called the front desk.

"May I help you?"

"Yes, this is Jerry Yang. My room has several problems. Would it be possible to move me to another?"

"I'm sorry, sir, but you're already in one of our better rooms."

I laughed.

I don't think the desk clerk caught the joke.

"Can you at least send up a television remote that works?"

"Coming right up, sir."

Nothing could dampen my excitement. I wanted to get to the Rio as quickly as possible. Before taking the fifteen-minute drive south on the expressway, though, I stopped at a drugstore and bought a large can of air freshener. Then I went back and emptied all of the contents into my room: in the bathroom, on the drapes and carpets, all around the bed, even a little into the hallway outside my room. If it stunk, I sprayed air freshener on it.

Then I tossed the can in the trash, shut the door, and headed for my car.

When I first walked into the Amazon Room of the Rio, I felt like a four-year-old boy walking through the gates of Disneyland. The place was like a carnival. Brightly colored booths lined the walls, filled with every poker-related thing you could imagine. Everywhere I turned, I saw free giveaways: poker chips, water bottles, magazines, key chains—you name it. I grabbed a plastic bag and went from one booth to the next, collecting free stuff. This way, even if I busted out the first day, I'd have something to show for my time in Vegas.

Once my bag was full, I headed into the room where play

actually takes place. The first day was well under way, and I could feel the excitement in the room. Poker tables went in both directions as far as the eye could see. Giant posters hung on the walls, each one maybe 10 or 12 feet high, showing photographs of all thirty-eight main event champions.

I stood and stared at the giant photos of Johnny Chan, Doyle Brunson, and my favorite player, Chris Ferguson. On the far wall was the photo of Joe Hachem, who'd won the main event that had introduced me to poker two years before. In a sense, he was the one who'd gotten me started. Now here I was, a player, not a spectator, in the very room where he'd won over $5 million.

Like every other player who stands and gawks at the champions' photos, I let myself dream a little. *If only my picture could hang up there.*

Before I left the main area, I stepped out of the tourist mode and tried to think like a poker player. I wandered about and watched a few hands at different tables, making a mental note of where ESPN's cameras were, how the room was lit, the spacing between the tables, how the cards were dealt, even the conversations among the players. Basically, I wanted to become familiar with everything so that when I came back the next morning to play, I wouldn't be so in awe of my surroundings that I'd make a fool of myself.

Outside the playing area, I stepped back into the poker carnival. I wanted to meet some of my poker idols. I didn't have to wait long. Standing there in the hallway was Chris "Jesus" Ferguson. A crowd gathered, one after another taking pictures with him or asking for his autograph.

I waited my turn. At 6 feet 3 inches, Chris towered over me. "Mr. Ferguson," I said as I held out my hand, "I want to tell you what a thrill it is for me to meet you. I've watched you play on television many times and have learned many things about the game from you."

He politely thanked me. "Are you here as a player?"

"Yes, I am. I start tomorrow."

"Well, good luck to you then." He smiled.

Only after I walked away did I realize I'd forgotten to ask him for an autograph.

Back at my hotel room, I found another surprise waiting for me. The musty, old, wet towel and cigarette stench had now become the musty, old, wet towel, cigarette, *and air freshener* stench. No matter what the label on the can may have said, the spray didn't eliminate odors. It simply added to them.

At least I won't be tempted to oversleep. I laughed. *I just hope the smell doesn't follow me back to the Rio.*

The following morning, my eyes popped open before my alarm sounded. Though I tried to treat this like any other morning, my body didn't want to cooperate. Six hours before play began, the adrenaline was already flowing.

Get a hold of yourself, Jerry. You can't start on tilt. You'll be the first one out for sure if you do.

I tried reading my Bible and praying, but my mind wanted to wander.

For the next thirty minutes, I soaked under a cold shower.

The chilly water snapped me back to where I needed to be. Even after the shower, though, I could feel the tension building inside.

Rather than letting it take over, I sat in a chair, closed my eyes, and went back to Laos. My buddies and I were in our village. No guns boomed in the distance, and no planes flew overhead. The five of us ran the trail to our favorite swimming hole. A waterfall on the river not far from our village emptied into a wide spot and formed a pond. A vine hung from a tree on one side. I saw myself there, the Hmong Tom Sawyer once again, swinging from the vine, splashing and laughing with my friends.

By the time I opened my eyes in my smelly Las Vegas hotel room, all of my anxiety was gone. I was ready to play.

Sitting at a table in the Amazon Room with a stack of 20,000 in chips feels very different than wandering around the room like a tourist. I wasn't nervous, at least not in a fearful way. More than anything, I was excited. I glanced toward the champions' pictures hanging on the walls and saw the image of Chris "Jesus" Ferguson, 2000 WSOP champion. *And I got to meet him yesterday*, I thought. *That was so much fun.* And that's what I'd come here to do: have fun. Just getting here was a victory in itself.

Other players took their seats at my table. They all had a look of excitement and terror as if they were climbing onto a monster roller coaster.

"Hi. I'm Jerry," I said and offered my hand. "Where are you from? What do you do for a living? Have you been playing poker for a long time? How have you enjoyed the World Series experience? Is this your first year here?"

In all the tournaments I'd played, I had rarely asked so many questions. However, I had a reason for being so chatty. One player said he lived right there in Vegas. That told me he probably played a lot of poker. Another was from North Dakota, which indicated he probably didn't play quite as much. Since I had never competed against any of these people, I hoped to find any bit of information I could use to gain an advantage.

The dealer took his seat. Play was about to begin. I reached into my jacket pocket and pulled out a photograph of my children. *This is for you,* I thought; then I gave the photograph a little kiss before laying it beside my chip stack.

"Good luck charm, Jerry?" another player said.

"No, it's my family. I'm here for them." It was a message to my opponents. I hadn't come to mess around; I'd come to win.

"Dealers, begin." The announcement came through the public address system.

"Good luck, gentlemen," our dealer said and then dealt the first hand.

As I looked at the two cards in front of me, a sense of joy washed over me. *This is really happening.*

I watched as each player looked at their cards. Several were overly excited like me, but in a couple of them I also sensed fear. *Take them out first,* I thought. The adrenaline was flowing.

Each day of the main event is divided into five two-hour rounds with twenty-minute breaks between. As I mentioned, on any given day, Texas Hold 'Em can be 90 percent skill or

90 percent luck, and that especially holds true on the starting days of the World Series of Poker.

During my first round of the 2007 main event, the cards certainly fell my way. I drew pocket aces seven times. There was that number again: seven. I couldn't believe it. Seven sets of pocket aces on 7-7-07. I think God was telling me something.

The first two-hour round ended. Blinds increased. Another two hours flew by, then another. My 20,000 in chips kept growing.

"Wow, Lady Luck is sure on your side today," one of the players said.

I just smiled. Drawing pocket aces seven times in two hours was certainly lucky, but even after I quit drawing strong hands, I played very well.

When a player gets on this kind of roll, it does something to the others. They hesitate to go up against you, growing increasingly cautious with every card. There's a difference between patience and caution. The latter gives the aggressive player a huge advantage, and I used it for all it was worth, bullying players into folding good hands.

I did not take silly chances or play loose, however. Some players will loosen up when they get on a roll and play hands they normally wouldn't. It doesn't take too many bad hands for a roll to turn into a bust. I stayed patient, picking my spots carefully, not taking foolish chances. No one ever won a main event on the first day, but over 3,000 were sure to lose.

A tone sounded, and an announcement came through the public address system telling us play had ended for the day.

The dealer at each table handed out bags with plastic seals on top. Each player counted his chips and recorded the amount along with his name and hometown on a slip of paper with two carbon copies underneath. One slip went in the bag, one went to the dealer, and one the player kept. Then the bags were sealed and locked away until the second round.

As I counted my chips, one player at my table said, "Wow, you have a lot of chips."

"Yeah, I guess I do."

"I'm not joking. I think you have a pretty good shot to cash out."

"Yeah, I did all right today."

Another player joined in. "How many do you have? Seventy, eighty thousand?"

"Ninety-nine thousand seven hundred."

"Whoa."

I fought the urge to take myself more seriously than I should. "You know, some days are like this. I just got lucky here and there."

"It takes more than luck to build up a stack like that at this place. You've got to be a pretty good player just to survive, much less get up around $100,000 on the first day."

"Thank you," I said as I finished writing. "You are very kind."

Later that night on the bed in my smelly hotel room, I re-played the events of the day. I thought about the hands I wished I'd played differently and plotted what I'd do the next time out.

The next time out. I smiled. *I'm going to have a next time in the World Series of Poker.* I laughed out loud. *Wow, I really do have a shot at going far in this thing. I can do this. I can compete here.*

I soaked up that thought for a few minutes. *This is unbelievable.*

Then I grabbed the phone and called Sue to give her the play-by-play of my day.

"Do you compete again tomorrow?"

"No, the last group has their opening day, so I have the day off. I don't go back until the second day of the second round."

"What are you going to do between now and then?"

"I'll go back to the Rio and get a few more autographs. But mainly, I have to get ready to play again."

After we talked a little while longer and said good night, I hung up and took a deep breath. *All right, Jerry, let's get focused here. It's time to plot strategy for the next round.*

Somewhere in the corner of the room, roaches scurried. Out on the street, a prostitute and a man, perhaps her pimp, yelled at one another. I hardly noticed. I had too much work to do.

9
Through the Jungle

Days turned into nights, nights into days as my family escaped through the jungle of Laos. When the sun rose, we found a place to eat and sleep. When the sun set, we broke camp and marched in the dark. Time had turned itself upside down and backward, which seemed appropriate. My life, the sense of comfort and familiarity that had wrapped around me since the day I was born, no longer existed. Why should time be any different?

I adjusted quickly to the strange new schedule. Going to sleep in the daylight came easily after walking all night.

We came upon an abandoned farm but couldn't risk staying in the house. Instead, my father led our group into a field just beyond the farm. He made a bed out of palm leaves for my brother and me. I could have slept standing. As soon as my head hit the leaves, I passed out.

When I awoke several hours later, I didn't experience the

jolt of reality I had the day we'd left. I didn't expect to see my house around me. I don't know why. I guess my mind had already turned loose of the familiar. Other children were already awake and playing. I didn't dare join them. My father warned my brothers, my sister, and me about making too much noise and giving away our position to the Communist soldiers.

I looked around the field for my father and finally spotted him on the edge of our camp. He leaned against a tree, his rifle across his lap. Even though all the men in our village took turns standing watch, my father couldn't bring himself to let his guard down even for a moment. While we were in the jungle, he never slept more than a couple hours at a time. Even then, he was always ready to spring into action with reflexes that must have been developed during his time in the army.

Daytime in our camp dragged on forever. I didn't have anything to do except wait . . . and wait . . . and wait. I occupied myself as well as I could. My older brother and I would help our mother by keeping our younger siblings content or getting things ready for a meal. With so little to eat, that chore didn't take long. I spent most of my time sitting on the ground tossing pebbles against a tree.

At least it was preferable to spending time among the people of my village. It's not that they did or said anything that made me want to keep my distance. No, the thing that frightened me, the one memory I cannot shake so many years later, is the look on their faces, especially the men's. All of these brave hunters, many of them former soldiers in General Vang Pao's army, sat in the field, waiting for darkness to fall, with terror in their eyes.

It wasn't just terror, though. Everyone, from the oldest man to the youngest child, wore an expression of despair. None of us had any illusions about the situation we faced or bright hopes for tomorrow. No, we wondered if we would live to see the next day.

From time to time during the long days of waiting, my buddies and I got together. We wanted to be as we had been just one week earlier, back in our village, when our only concern was how to have fun.

Sitting in a jungle camp, waiting for the sun to set, none of us felt like having fun. We didn't laugh. We didn't joke. Honestly, we pretty much just sat there and stared at one another. Once or twice one of them pointed at a long scratch on my arm and said something like, "Did that hurt?" or we held up our feet and compared cuts and scars. After a while, we drifted back to our families to prepare for another night of walking through the jungle.

Though we had no choice but to eat random leaves on the trail, I came to regret it. A sharp pain hit low in my stomach. "I don't feel so good," I told Xay, who was walking in front of me.

"Me either."

I kept walking. I didn't have a choice, but the sharp pain grew stronger. I had never been so thankful for anything in my life than when my father finally let us take a brief rest stop. I darted off to one side, found a secluded spot, and relieved myself.

The pain didn't go away. In fact, it stayed with me the rest of the way. I wasn't the only one who got it. If I had to guess, I would say most of the children and a good number of the adults came down with diarrhea within our first couple of nights on the trail.

To make it to the Mekong without getting caught by the Communists, we needed to move as quickly as possible. As more and more people got sick, we had to stop more often and for longer periods of time.

Keep in mind, we were walking through the jungle, hiding in the dark, doing our best not to be discovered by the Communist soldiers patrolling the area. It wasn't like we could go home, lie down, and let the ailment run its course. We didn't have Pepto-Bismol to pass around, and there weren't any rest stops in the jungle. Throw in the oppressive heat and humidity, and you're left with a miserable group of people.

The next night, I walked along the trail, holding on to my brother's shirt as he walked in front of me. My stomach hurt, my feet ached, and all I wanted was to find a quiet place, lie down, and go to sleep. All of a sudden, a piercing cry shot through the jungle. I nearly jumped out of my skin. Then another answered it from the other side of the trail.

Before I could ask what was going on, a dark shape flew past. I screamed. Another dark shape swung by and another and another.

Small children cried. Adults let out startled screams.

I started to lose my hold on my brother's shirt and wanted to take off running, but the thought of getting lost in the jungle frightened me more than the dark shapes.

Another dropped to the ground close to me, and I could finally see what was getting everyone so upset: monkeys. A troop of fifteen or twenty had dropped from their usual spots in the tops of trees, and we'd walked right into the middle of them.

My brother turned and laughed at me. "You screamed like a little girl over nothing but a monkey. We've eaten monkeys for dinner."

He kept laughing, and I laughed with him.

Apparently a lot of the families in the village had eaten monkey. The startled screams turned into shouts of "Let's shoot them and eat them."

"No, don't shoot," my father yelled. "Do you want every soldier in the whole country to come running? How stupid can you be? That gunshot will echo for miles. Just leave them alone, and let's keep going." My father truly was a great leader, not allowing our empty bellies to distract us from our primary objective.

The monkeys kept jumping around and scaring the children, but we continued walking. We had a lot of ground to cover that night.

The mood in the camp took a sharp turn. On the third or fourth day, I woke up to the sound of that distinctive death cry I'd grown to fear. People ran past me, so I jumped up and followed them. The crowd stopped, but I was small enough to push through and see exactly what was going on.

Once I finally made it to the front of the crowd, I saw a young mother sitting on the ground, rocking back and forth, wailing, clutching her two-year-old son. Her husband stood behind her, and even though he tried to keep it together, he started making the cry himself.

My village was small. Everyone knew each other, and I knew this family. They lived near our house. Even though he was much younger than me, I'd played with this little boy. In my mind, I could still see him running and laughing like a normal two-year-old. He'd had the same kind of stomach virus that had plagued most of the people in our camp. I'm pretty sure he'd been sick already before we'd started through the jungle and didn't have the strength in his little body to fight off the illness that was ravaging our camp. His mother had awakened and found him lying next to her, cold.

The cry grew louder as other people mourned with the boy's mother and father.

The wailing didn't exactly fit into our plan of blending into the jungle to avoid the Communist patrols. My father took control of the situation. "No, don't cry. You have to be strong. We'll give you some time to spend with the child. After that, we'll help find a place to bury him."

A couple hours later, the men from the camp carried the boy's body to a secluded place away from our camp. The parents wrapped their baby in palm leaves and laid him in the ground. After covering him, we placed large rocks over the grave to keep the animals from disturbing it.

I wish I could say this was the last fatality during our escape through the jungle. It wasn't. Nine or ten people from my village never made it to the Mekong River.

The first death, though, was the worst.

When the sun went down, we headed out, walking through the jungle as usual. No one had to remind us to be quiet. No one talked or made a sound of any kind. The whole demeanor of our people had changed. Everyone was so sad, even more hopeless than before.

The pains in my stomach returned, as they did for a lot of people. On our next stop, a few people complained of fever. Our march turned into more of a shuffle. I thought we would never make it out of the jungle.

The rains came, making the jungle even darker. On the clear nights, the moon and stars gave us enough light to distinguish the trail from the trees. Once the rain came, though, I could barely see my hand. And the rain made it so cold.

But worse were the leeches.

Before normal life had ended, my parents would bring a small bag of salt whenever we traveled through the jungle. If a leech attached itself to one of us, my mother or father would drop a little salt on it, and the leech would fall away.

On this trip, we didn't have extra room for salt.

The rain made the leeches pop out everywhere. In the dark, I couldn't see them; I could only feel them. When we finally stopped for our first short rest of the night, I threw off my clothes and found four leeches in the worst possible place for a boy to find them.

The rain started pouring in sheets. The narrow path grew slick with mud. I slipped and fell again and again. All around me, little children cried.

Finally, my father said, "We can't keep going like this. We need to find a place to camp until the rains stop."

Before long, we came upon a steep cliff with a sharp outcrop of rock that looked a little like an awning.

"This will work," my father said. "All the women and children can get out of the rain here. Everyone else, take shelter under the palm trees."

As strange as it may sound, finding that rock changed my whole outlook on the trip. I knew it was more than a coincidence that we found it. In all our days of walking through the jungle, we never saw anything like it again. It was as though God placed that rock there just for us right at the moment we needed it. I saw it as an answer to prayer. We prayed a lot on this journey. My father said a prayer with every step he took.

I tried to sleep, but I was so cold and soaked to the skin. I huddled against my mother.

The jungle was completely silent, except for the sound of the rain and children whimpering.

In the darkness, my ears perked.

Someone had mentioned my father's name.

"I don't think Youa Lo and the others know what they're doing. We should have made it to the Mekong by now."

Someone agreed. "We should have stayed home and taken our chances with the Communists." Then the person cursed my father and the other leaders of our village.

I wanted to jump up and tell them we would all be dead by now if it weren't for my father. I wanted to tell them everyone should stop whining and work together and help make life easier for all of us. I wanted to say a lot of things, but little boys weren't supposed to speak up.

Instead, I pulled closer to my mother and prayed the rain would soon end.

The next morning, the rains finally stopped. We camped under the rock until the sun went down, then started walking. Again.

The pain in my feet and legs grew so severe I couldn't take another step. My father swept me up and placed me on his shoulders, all the while carrying my baby brother in a basket in one hand. My grandmother carried my younger brother, and one of my aunts carried my sister. Somehow, my oldest brother managed to keep walking.

On the sixth or seventh day (it's hard to say which because the days and nights all blended together in the jungle), we reached the end of our bamboo thermos supply of pork, and we were nearly out of rice. The meager portions my father had handed out to us the first couple of days had been like a Thanksgiving feast in comparison. Now we needed to rely even more on whatever we could find.

At this point, we ate anything even remotely edible. Having to forage for food slowed us even more. The sight of an animal brought the entire group to a halt so that the men could try to trap or shoot it with one of their crossbows. I ate tree frogs, monkey—anything.

Our group began breaking down. People hoarded food, and everyone became focused on themselves. Arguments sprang up. More people criticized my father and the other elders.

The trip had taken much longer than anyone had anticipated, making matters worse. Traveling only at night was no longer an option. My father knew our group couldn't survive much longer, so he took the chance of heading out, even in the daylight.

On about the eighth day, we were getting close to the river and closer to the Pathet Lao and NVA. The most direct route to the Mekong went right into the heart of the fighting. We had no choice but to take a long, winding path around a mountain.

With so many Communist soldiers in the area, my father thought it best to split our group in two in hopes that even if some of us were caught, at least the others might make it to the river and across to Thailand. Half of us went around the right side of the mountain; the other half around the left. The plan was for both groups to make it around the mountain by nightfall.

Most of the jungle paths we'd followed up till this point had been little more than animal trails. Occasionally, we'd come across a hunting trail or a small road, but those had been rare. Around this mountain, we couldn't locate any kind of trail. My father and uncles had to blaze one by hacking through the brush with machetes.

We couldn't stop. For all we knew, the Communist soldiers had an outpost high on the mountain to watch the valley below and could come at us from any direction.

No sooner had we started around the mountain than a widow ran up to my father carrying her child. The boy looked dead to me, until he made a low cry. I'd been around enough death already to know he probably wouldn't make it. I knew this boy from back in our village. He was maybe a year younger than me.

"My child is dying," his mother said. "He needs something warm to eat."

The child had grown so weak that he couldn't eat solid food. In Laos, the women used to make a soup out of rice for those too sick for solid food. The widow wanted to make this for her son.

"I'm sorry, but we cannot risk building a fire to cook something warm for your son. Besides, we have to keep moving. We can't stop or we'll get caught."

"You don't understand." Tears ran down the mother's face. "He's going to die if we don't do something. *Please*. I love my baby. He's all I have left in the world. You cannot just let him die."

I don't know how my father held it together. He looked at her little boy lying lifelessly in her arms. "I understand," he said softly, "but I am sorry. We cannot risk everyone's lives to save the life of one child. If we save him but give ourselves away to the Communists, we may all die."

The woman sobbed. "I have to save my son."

"I'm sorry, but we have to keep moving."

My grandmother stepped up and took the woman by the arm. She and some of the other women in our group gathered what rice we had left, crushed it, and mixed it with water. They then tried to feed it to the dying child, but he didn't respond.

To this day I can still hear the sound of that mother crying softly. "My son is dying. My son is dying."

I wish I could get it out of my ears.

Six hours later, we made it to the far side of the mountain. I looked at the boy in his mother's arms. I didn't think he was breathing.

My father walked to her and laid his hands on the child. "Okay, I think we can risk building a small fire but only for a moment."

The mother hardly responded as she sat there, slowly rocking her son.

While some of the women prepared the rice soup, my grandmother gathered some roots and ground them into a powder. "Here, this will help him." Though we didn't have doctors in Hmong villages, my grandmother and others like her knew which herbs to give as medicine.

The other half of our group soon joined us. No one had seen them as they'd passed along the far side of the mountain.

Everyone was exhausted from the long day and night of hiking through thick underbrush. "We will rest here," my father announced, "and then leave when the sun sets. Get some rest. We will make it to the river soon."

Not long ago, I visited the sick, dying boy. He lives in Florida with his wife and family. I nearly broke down when I saw him. It's a miracle he survived the jungle.

All we needed was one or two more miracles, and we would be safely out of Laos. Unfortunately, we'd already used up our quota.

10
Caught!

From the time I was a very little boy, I had lived in fear of the Pathet Lao and North Vietnamese soldiers, wondering when a squad of soldiers would rush into our village and kill us all. Other villages had suffered this fate.

I felt even more at risk escaping through the jungle. I didn't have a warm feeling deep inside reassuring me we would make it to the Mekong and the safety of Thailand.

My terror grew stronger with each passing day. I knew the longer it took us to get to the river, the more likely it was that we'd get caught.

During the daylight hours of about the ninth day, we had rested. Now it was getting dark. Soon we'd break camp for what I hoped would be the last time. The land had flattened out, and the jungle was much less dense.

We were close to the river. Everyone knew it, which made us all the more anxious. Having come so far, we still had a long way to go before any of us could relax.

I overheard my father tell one of my uncles we needed to hire boats to take us across the Mekong.

The fact that they were seriously discussing it made my hopes soar. *Perhaps we can cross tonight!*

"We must be careful not to be seen even on the river," my father warned. "The boats we hire must be small enough to appear no more menacing than fishing boats out for the night."

My father and the other leaders walked throughout our camp and asked all the families, "How much money do you have?"

A few families carried a small amount of paper money. Others had one or two silver bars, and some owned nothing of value except the traditional family necklace handed down from generation to generation. That necklace constituted some families' life savings. All of them gave up what they had to safely cross the Mekong.

We didn't have much, but after surveying the contributions everyone made, my father felt we had more than enough to hire the boats. Unfortunately, having enough money to hire someone to ferry us across the river was only one part of the equation.

Every day of our journey, I'd heard fighting in the distance. Now that we were close to the river, the sounds intensified.

"The Communist and Thai armies are shooting at one another across the river," my father explained to me.

"Why? Are the Communists going to take over Thailand, too?"

"No, the Americans will never leave Thailand, which means it will always be safe."

"Then why are they shooting?"

"The Communists are trying to stop people like us from crossing the river."

I later came to understand that the Pathet Lao didn't simply want to keep everyone they could in their country. Rather, they wanted to ensure their silence. Those who escaped carried their horror stories with them. As more Hmong and other Lao made it to freedom in Thailand, more stories of abuse at the hands of the Communists surfaced. That, along with the Pathet Lao's desire for revenge against their enemies, explained why these soldiers fought so hard to force people to stay.

All of this meant we had to carefully choose where we approached the Mekong. If we picked the wrong place, we might very well walk right into a Pathet Lao camp.

Just as I'd started to feel hopeful about our escape, it dawned on me that the most dangerous part of our journey lay ahead.

Before we resumed, my father and the other men in our group huddled together and decided to get rid of all our weapons.

"We don't want the people with the boats to think we pose a threat to them," my father said.

Two men dug a shallow pit, and the men threw in every weapon except one rifle, which my father carried.

This decision may well have saved our lives later, but at the time it made me more than a little nervous. *How will we protect ourselves if we run into some soldiers?* I wondered.

As soon as the sun set, we broke camp. With all the talk

of hiring boats to ferry us across the river, I just knew this was the night we would finally make it to Thailand. Everyone sensed it.

Our pace picked up. Instead of walking, it was as though we were running down the path. Looking back, I know we weren't, not with so many children and so much sickness in our group. Yet compared to the snail's pace we had been reduced to, even walking fast felt like sprinting.

The area was crisscrossed with roads and highways, so we had to walk in quick bursts. While hidden in brush, we walked parallel to the roads. Though I had never in my life yet seen a car, I heard vehicles driving by.

No matter how much we tried to stay out of sight, eventually we always came to a road that had to be crossed. Especially when it was wide, this was extremely dangerous. Rather than risking all 100 of us dashing across at once, my father sent us in groups of five to ten.

Each group ran as fast as their legs would go. Once across, they dove into the brush and motioned for the next. More than once, we heard cars coming when only half of the group was across. All of us sank into the bushes and waited for vehicles to pass. Then the next group ran across and the next and the next until we were all safely across.

The second time we raced across a road, I tripped. We still had a small supply of rice, which I was carrying in a bag on my back. When I fell, the rice sprayed across the roadway.

My father didn't say anything. He didn't have to. His expression said it all.

I scrambled to my feet, scooped up as much rice as I could, then ran to safety.

After hiking all night, we found ourselves about 30 miles from Vientiane. We had to cross even more roads and dodge more cars and trucks.

The eastern sky grew bright with the rising sun, but my father didn't want to stop. "We're too close to town to find a place to camp for the day. Let's keep going."

The trail ran alongside a small road. We needed to cross it but had to look for the right place. Finally we came upon a large stand of bamboo.

"Everybody hide here," my father said. "I'll make sure there aren't any cars, and then we'll cross."

He and a couple of my uncles crept out of the bamboo in opposite directions. A few minutes later, they returned. "This looks like a good spot," my father said. "The road is narrow, and we seem to be in a pretty isolated place. Let's get across as fast as we can."

Because the road was so small and secluded, my father sent several groups across at once. The first thirty moved out of the bamboo and set foot on the pavement.

Two trucks pulled up so fast that none of us could do anything. As strange as it may sound, the sight of those trucks made me excited and terrified at the same time. The little boy in me thought they were the neatest things I'd ever seen. Never had I been near a machine so large, powerful, and mesmerizing.

And then I saw the soldiers. My excitement turned to dread.

The trucks zoomed past, and for a moment I thought perhaps they hadn't noticed the large group of Hmong people dressed in rags and carrying on their backs everything they had in the world.

My hope was dashed when the trucks skidded to a stop. A squad of soldiers jumped out of the back and ran directly toward us, waving their guns.

We stopped dead in our tracks.

The soldiers screamed, some speaking Lao, others Vietnamese. Finally we heard, "Freeze! Don't move."

Believe me, I couldn't have moved a muscle even if I'd wanted to. My body was frozen in fear. From the moment we'd left our village, I'd lived in constant dread of this very moment. My nightmare had come true.

Before the soldiers reached us, my father stepped forward to let them know he was our leader. Falling to his knees, he bowed toward the soldiers. "Please, please, sirs, we mean you no harm."

Two of my uncles threw themselves on the ground and joined him in pleading for our lives.

The soldiers ignored them. "Who's in there?" one yelled and pointed his gun toward the bamboo brush where the rest of our group was hiding. "Get out. Show yourselves *now.*"

One by one, people slowly walked out of the bamboo until everyone was out in the open on the road. All the while, the soldiers screamed at us.

Some of the mothers began crying as they held their children close. Many in our group spoke Hmong only and didn't understand anything the soldiers said. Those who spoke Lao began to beg.

"Please don't hurt my child."

"Please don't hurt us."

Aggravated, the soldiers waved their guns, pointing them in one direction and then another. They spread out, surrounded us, and raised their guns as if they were going to open fire.

One particular soldier aimed his gun directly at my head, the tip of the barrel maybe a foot from my nose.

My father had taught me all about guns. He'd said, "You never place your finger on the trigger unless you intend to shoot."

Dressed in rags, a bag of rice on my back, no shoes on my feet, I stood in front of that soldier and watched him place his finger directly on the trigger of his AK-47.

I wanted to cry but refused. Instead, I stood as still as I could, the gun so close I could smell the oil on the barrel. I didn't even blink; my gaze stayed glued to his finger on the trigger.

"Please," my father repeated, "we mean you no harm."

"Then why do you carry guns?" the squad commander replied, finally acknowledging my father's presence.

"For hunting and for our safety. Our country is at war. There is much instability now. I need to protect my family. I'm breaking no laws by carrying a gun. Besides, we have so few guns among so many people. Surely that must show you we are no real threat to anyone."

"Shut up," the squad commander shouted. "We know what you're up to. You're betraying your homeland and fleeing to Thailand."

The soldier pointing the AK-47 at my head appeared to

become agitated. His finger twitched on the trigger while his eyes darted back and forth across our entire group.

"No, no, no," my father said.

"Don't lie to me. Do you think we're stupid? Do you expect me to believe so many people decided to go out for an early morning stroll carrying all their possessions? You're trying to cross the Mekong and get to Thailand. We should just shoot you on the spot if that's the way you feel about the land that's done so much for you."

"No, I beg of you, no. It's true we left our home in the mountains. But we did so to start new lives here in the valley, where the land is better. We could never leave our homeland. I know you're good men and you have brought us a good government. You'll make our country more stable and successful. Just as you have given our country a new beginning, we seek one as well."

"You lie."

"No, my lord," my father said, bowing low, "I give you my word that I am not."

"Then where are you headed? What town do you plan to move to?"

My father had to name a town quickly or the squad commander would know he was lying. Without hesitation, he said, "Num Chang."

"Num Chang, eh? Why Num Chang? Do you know someone there?"

"My uncle Ying Yang lives there."

"We don't believe you, and we don't have time to argue with you."

Out of the corner of my eye, I could see my father face-down on the ground.

The soldier in front of me appeared to pull his gun tighter against his shoulder as if preparing to fire.

This is it, Xao. In that moment, I fully expected to die.

Instead of ordering his men to fire, though, the commander said, "Here's what I want you to do. My commanding officer is in Hin Haw. You're going to go there and plead your case with him. I don't have time to mess with you. He'll decide what's to be done with you."

Hin Haw? Anywhere but Hin Haw! News that the Pathet Lao had attacked Hin Haw is what had prompted the people of my village to flee toward the Mekong in the first place. Now we were being sent there. I couldn't believe my ears.

My father tried to talk the squad commander out of making us walk all the way to Hin Haw. "Please, please, just let my people go. It's such a long walk, and we have so many small children."

No matter what my father said, the squad commander refused to listen. "There is no way out. You have to go or else."

I felt the tension building. The squad commander seemed to be running out of patience. I could tell that all of the soldiers were anxious to get back in their trucks and get on to wherever it was they were going.

"Thank you, my lord," my father said. "Yes, of course, we will do whatever you need us to do. We will go to Hin Haw as quickly as we can."

The squad commander shouted an order to his men, who lowered their guns. Only then did I notice I hadn't taken a breath in a very long time.

Even today, I don't know why that squad of soldiers allowed us to live. I give all the credit to God. I know without a doubt He was with us and changed the squad commander's heart. I have no other explanation for why I'm still alive.

I also credit my father. By showing such great respect for the soldiers, he defused the volatile situation. The squad commander was waiting for a reason, no matter how flimsy, to order his men to open fire. My father stayed calm and didn't give him one.

However, though we were saved for now, our hazardous journey was far from over.

The squad commander left one truck behind to escort us to Hin Haw. Soldiers rode in the back of the truck, their guns pointed in our direction. None of them appeared to be in any hurry to pull the trigger or to get anywhere fast. About four or five soldiers walked alongside us.

"Do you mind if some of our small children ride in your truck?" my father asked. "Then we can make it to Hin Haw much faster and free you from wasting time on those as insignificant as us."

"No," a soldier snapped. "You walk."

The journey passed much more quickly than I'd thought possible. In a little more than half a day, we made it to Hin Haw. The same distance through the jungle would have taken several days. Even so, I preferred the latter.

With my every step toward Hin Haw, a feeling of absolute terror came over me. Everyone in our group knew all the stories of how the Communists had wiped out most of the people in that village. The pain in my feet went away. I was too worried to think about something as trivial as a few cuts.

Everyone in our group had the same feelings I did. No one talked as we walked along the road to Hin Haw. The only sounds were the shuffling of our feet on the road and the cries of little children and their mothers.

We arrived in Hin Haw at about three in the afternoon. A large dirt field spread before us. Trucks moved in and out, filling the air with red dust. As we moved closer, large groups like ours were being herded at gunpoint. Fathers, mothers, and little children were forced into the trucks. Men argued with the soldiers, trying to convince them to free their families. The soldiers didn't listen but kept prodding the people forward with their guns and throwing them on the trucks. Once the trucks were full, they drove away, kicking up even more red dirt.

"What's going on over there?" my father asked the soldier walking next to him.

"These people are being taken back home to their villages," he replied.

Judging by the people's faces and the cries coming from the trucks, I doubted he was telling us the complete story.

The soldiers led our group to a small wooden house with a corrugated tin roof. "Wait here."

We stopped but didn't dare sit. Standing as still as we could, we waited for further instructions.

From my position beside my father, I looked all around. Off to the side of the wooden house, the ground was stained red with blood and littered with pieces of flesh and bones and organs. A little farther, black and blue plastic sheets covered the ground, blood seeping outward from under them. The sheets appeared to be covering bodies. Lots and lots of bodies.

No wonder these people didn't want to get in the trucks. Had this been the squad commander's plan all along? To torture our minds with the hope of being saved, only to send us here to be shot like dogs?

I looked at my father, whose eyes were fixed on the plastic sheets and bloodstains. He glanced at my uncles. "When the commander comes out, do what I do," he said softly.

Two hours went by as we stood in the sun, exhausted. Finally, the door of the small wooden house opened, and the commanding officer appeared.

The moment he stepped out, my father fell to his knees and began begging for the life of every person in his village. You must understand, my father is a strong, proud man. Before this day, my mind could not imagine the sight of my father on the ground pleading for anything from anyone. He was, and is, my greatest hero. Yet here he was, crying like a small child, my uncles following his lead. "Please let my people go."

The commanding officer walked down the two steps of the wooden house and stood over my father, two soldiers on either side of him. Arrogance rolled off of him. Wearing a Pathet Lao dress uniform, he had a pistol strapped to his side. The soldiers next to him held AK-47s with bright red wooden gun stocks.

He looked at my father, sneering. "I know what you're doing. You're just trying to save yourself. Vang Pao"—he sort of spit out the name, as if he'd tasted something bitter—"already ran away to Thailand, and you want to go be with him. What's the matter with you? Do you understand Vang Pao and the Americans were using you? They didn't care about you. They cared nothing about our country. To them, you were nothing but a slimy little worm."

"Yes, my lord." My father's gaze never rose from the ground.

"We care about this country," the commanding officer said. "We want to build it up, to make it a better place. Don't you understand that?"

Even though he lectured him as one would an ignorant child, my father responded with respect. "Yes, my lord, I understand what you are saying, and I agree with you. I love this country. My ancestors came here a long time ago. Why would I want to go to a place I don't know? My land is here; my children are here. Why would I want to leave?"

"Then why are you trying to get to the Mekong?"

"No, my lord. We are not on our way to the Mekong. We left our homes in the mountains to make a new life for ourselves on the plains where the land is better. We were on our way to Num Chang when your soldiers stopped us."

"Why Num Chang? Do you know someone there?"

"Of course, my lord. My uncle Ying Yang lives there with his wife."

I saw the commander's eyes light up when my father mentioned my uncle's wife. Her brother had been a high-ranking officer in the Royal Lao Army before defecting to the Pathet Lao. "No, I don't believe you. And even if Ying Yang is your uncle as you say, we are not going to let you go to Num Chang. You and all your people will be sent back to your village."

My father didn't back down. The bodies under the tarps and the horror stories of Hmong sent off to reeducation camps made him refuse to allow any of us to be placed on one of the trucks in the field of red dirt. "No, please, please don't do that. There is no life for us back in the mountains. How could you send my people back to a place where we have no hope? Please allow us to start a new life in the valley. Life was so hard in the mountains. We want to plant our rice in the open fields rather than chopping the forests year after year. The reason we came from the mountains was that we heard some people in the valley had already betrayed our country and fled across the Mekong, leaving their farms behind. We came to take over their fields."

I could tell by the look on the commander's face that he didn't believe a word of it. Eyes narrowing, body stiffening, he said, "Don't you lie to me. How dare you speak to me in such a disrespectful way? Do you think I'm stupid? Do you think I don't know what you're trying to do here? You're trying to pull a fast one. The moment I let you go, you and your people will go straight to the Mekong. Well, you won't get the chance. You and your people will get in the trucks right now."

Refusing to take no for an answer, my father kept pleading.

Then something miraculous happened. As though his heart had been touched by God, the commander's demeanor changed and he said to my father, "Okay, you and your people can go to Num Chang. However, I'm going to send my men in a few days, and they'd better find you there. If they don't, I will hunt you myself. No matter where I find you, that place will be your grave."

"Of course, my lord. You can count on us. I would consider it a great honor to have you as my guest. Our home is your home."

"Get out of my sight." The commander waved at my father as if he were swatting at a fly. He snorted something to his men, then spun on his heels and went back into his house.

I knew without a doubt that we shouldn't have survived this day, the one I'd feared above all others. Instead of lying dead on that red field, though, we were walking toward Num Chang, a town near the Mekong. My father had even managed to convince the commander to give us a letter of passage to make sure no other soldiers harassed us.

Though we were far from the Mekong, a sense of hope came over me. I didn't know how or when, but for the first time, I started to believe we would actually make it to Thailand and freedom. If we could survive this day, we could survive anything.

11

Across the Mekong

We arrived in Num Chang early in the morning after a long night's walk. For me, the worst part of the trip had been traveling through Hin Haw on our way out of town. Trucks filled with soldiers had driven past. When the soldiers had spotted us, they'd shot into the sky to intimidate us. Other trucks filled with Hmong or Lao families had zipped by on their way to God knows where. The cries in those trucks—that distinctive Hmong sound of mourning—had made me shudder, knowing that could have easily been my family.

Even without the trucks, Hin Haw had frightened me. Gutted cars had littered the streets. Bullet holes had riddled houses. Blood had stained the roads and sidewalks.

My father could see the fear in my eyes. "Don't look here or there, Xao. Keep your eyes on the road right in front of you."

I'd done my best to follow my father's instructions. Even then, smoke had stung my nose, and the roars and cries of passing trucks had filled my ears. From time to time, I'd had to walk around drying blood.

We reached Num Chang before sunrise and didn't have any trouble finding places to stay. Large sections of the town were completely abandoned. The houses had the same tell-tale signs that a battle had recently been fought here: bullet holes covered the walls, and some places were bombed out completely. Cars and trash littered the streets here, too.

Even after the sun came up, we saw few people in this fairly large town. Most had either escaped to Thailand, died at the hands of the Communists, or been sent away to reeducation camps. The few who remained stayed out of sight.

Many of the streets of Num Chang were lined with palm trees. For some reason, I cannot forget those trees. All of them had bullet holes up and down the trunks. *Why would anyone waste so many bullets shooting up palm trees?* I will never forget one in particular. Lodged there in the trunk at exactly my eye level was a bullet. *That would have hit me in the head if I'd been standing here.*

My family moved into an abandoned house. It seemed the residents had left in a big hurry. Someone had spilled rice across the dirt floor of the main room and taken off without scooping it up. My mother dug every grain out of the floor, rinsed it, and cooked it for us. We searched every corner of the house for hidden food but didn't find any more. Some dishes were still there, not the good ones, but the kind nobody wanted. Even the gardens behind the abandoned houses had been picked clean. Anything of value not carried off by the fleeing people had been pillaged by the soldiers.

And there were lots of them in Num Chang. Soldiers sped through the streets at all hours, firing their guns into the sky just as those in Hin Haw had. Most looked more like teenage boys, and their highest form of entertainment appeared to be scaring us.

My father and uncles went to the local market to try to buy food. At least that's what they said they were doing.

My father knew our lives were in serious danger. The Pathet Lao commander could change his mind at any moment. Even if he forgot about us, it was simply a matter of time before one of the other bands of soldiers patrolling the town decided they were tired of the sight of such a large group of dirty, smelly Hmong dressed in their mountain rags. Even before the fall of the Royal Lao family, the Lao people who lived on the plains had looked down on the Hmong.

My father and uncles, knowing they had to act fast, used their trips to the area markets as a way of gathering news about the war and the Communist soldiers' locations near the Mekong.

During one of these trips to the market in a nearby town, my father came in contact with an old relative, a Yang just like us. He, too, had once served as an officer in General Vang Pao's army but felt he couldn't leave Laos because he had brothers who were part of the Pathet Lao.

When this old relative offered to help us, at first my father refused his assistance. Time and again, my father said, "You are wrong about us. We don't want to go to Thailand. We love Laos and are perfectly content to stay here."

"I know you don't mean that," the man replied. "Let me help you. I must. I cannot bear the thought of you being dragged away by the soldiers."

With little time and nowhere else to turn, my father finally decided to trust him.

"Here's what I'll do for you," the relative said. "I'll provide trucks to take you and all of your people to the Mekong. I also know two men with boats who will agree to ferry you across the river to Thailand."

"I want to see these boats and meet the men before I risk the lives of my family."

"Of course."

Later that week, my father and two of my uncles traveled to the Mekong with the man. Secretly, before their scouting mission, my father told my uncles, "If his story checks out, we'll pay any price they want. But if you sense something isn't right with this guy, eliminate him right away, before he can turn us in to the authorities."

Thankfully the man's story checked out and the boats were hired.

"Tomorrow night we leave," my father announced.

I was elated and scared to death.

In order to slip out of town unnoticed, we planned to leave around two or three in the morning. The relative told my father to have us walk on the main road. Once we were out of town, a pair of trucks would pass us, then double back to pick us up. They would drive us to the Mekong River, where we would hide until the next night. Then boats would ferry us across at the next sundown.

The plan seemed foolproof until the Pathet Lao and NVA soldiers in town decided to hold a party in a large field not far from the main road. The moment the sun set, the celebration kicked off.

I could see the bonfires from my house, and the music was so loud I felt as if I was at the event myself. I looked out my window and saw the soldiers dancing with a bunch of women. Every so often, they shot their guns into the sky and laughed and danced some more. It was the biggest party I had ever seen. From the looks of things, it would last all night.

Unfortunately, we had no way of contacting our relative and telling him to scrub the plans for our escape. If the trucks came this night, they would drive right into a large group of drunk and trigger-happy soldiers.

I couldn't sleep even if I wanted to. None of us could. I walked into the main room of the house where we were staying and found my father and mother on their knees, praying.

"God, help us," my father said. "We must leave tonight, but we cannot because of these men. Please do something. We need Your protection, Your guidance."

I got on my knees and joined them. I was so scared; I didn't know what else to do.

Even though we'd faced many hardships during our escape, I knew God was with us. He'd led us to a shelter in the jungle when the rains had come, and He'd delivered us from the soldiers when we'd been caught.

On this night, He sent another miracle. The soldiers' party had just become even wilder when all of a sudden, the skies opened and sheets of rain fell. The soldiers and party women went scrambling, looking for someplace dry.

Almost instantaneously, the fires went out, the music stopped, and the night became completely silent, except for the sound of the pouring rain.

Sometime around three in the morning, as the rain still fell outside, my father gathered us. "It's time. Let's go."

As quietly as we could, everyone from our village slipped into the main street of Num Chang and headed out of town. Half an hour later, a set of headlights came toward us.

"Move to the sides and keep walking," my father said.

I didn't quite understand why. If these weren't the trucks that were supposed to take us to the Mekong, we should have jumped off the road and hidden. If they were the trucks, we should have stopped and let them pick us up.

One truck then another drove past us, headed in the opposite direction. A few minutes later, I glanced back and saw headlights coming from behind us.

My father saw them, too. "Stay on the road and run as fast as you can."

The headlights turned out to belong to the same two trucks that had sped past us a few minutes earlier. Instead of passing us again, the two trucks slowed. One of the drivers rolled down his window and shouted something to my father.

"Don't stop," my father called. "Keep running and jump

into the trucks." Then he yelled, "Get in the trucks *now*."

Chaos ensued. Parents tossed their children into the trucks, then dove in after them.

My father jogged alongside, my baby brother on his back and my older brother just in front of him. "Hurry, hurry!" He kept running along, making sure everyone was in one of the two trucks before he climbed in.

My mother, sister, other brother, and I dove into the second truck. As soon as I landed in the back, I turned around to help with my little brother. Suddenly, the trucks hit the gas and sped up.

"No, wait!" I yelled, but it was too late. I watched my father, my baby brother, and my older brother disappear into the darkness. I feared I would never see them again.

Just in time, our old relative looked back from the front of one of the vehicles to see my father running desperately in the rain. The truck slowed down.

My father later told me how it felt to see the fading tail-lights of the two trucks: it was the worst moment of his life.

We drove through the night. As our vehicle rocked along the bumpy road, I tried to sleep, but my growling stomach kept me awake. Rain beat constantly on the tarp covering the truck bed.

I must have dozed off because the next thing I knew, the driver was shouting, "Out, out, out. Everybody out!"

As the sun rose, I jumped out of the truck with my family.

The moment my feet hit the ground, my father yelled, "Follow me. Quickly. Run!"

With no time to look around, I found myself racing down a steep hill, across a rice field, past a couple of houses, and into a small hut surrounded by tall grass, bamboo, and palm trees.

"We must wait here for the sun to set," my father said.

But the sun hasn't even come up yet, I thought.

Gunfire echoed outside as the Thai and Pathet Lao armies shot at one another from opposite sides of the Mekong. The little children in our group cried. Angry adults snapped: "Shut those kids up before you give us away."

I started to ask if I could have something to eat but stopped myself. No one had brought any food with them, since no one had really known how long it would take to get from Num Chang to the Mekong.

We couldn't go out without getting caught. We had no choice but to sit and wait. No food. No water. Nothing.

It was one of the longest days of my life.

Finally, night came. Just after dark, two men walked to the hut and said, "Come with us. We're here to take you across the river. Do you have the rest of the money?"

"Yes, of course," my father replied. "I will give it to you once we are safely across the river." My father had already given them half of the price he'd agreed to the day he'd come to the Mekong with the old relative.

"No, we want it now."

"After we cross the river."

"You give us the money now, or we will leave and you can swim across."

My father held his ground. "I will happily give you the rest of your money after the last person in our group steps on the Thai shore. That's what we agreed to."

For a moment I wondered if the two men with the boats were going to back out and walk away, leaving us stranded in this horrible little hut.

Finally, they gave in. "Okay, okay, whatever you want." I could tell they weren't happy with my father.

As the two men left to get their boats, my father gathered everyone from our village. A few friends of our old relative had also joined our group. They, too, wanted out of Laos.

"The boats cannot carry everyone at once," my father announced. "We're going to do the same thing we did when we crossed the roads in the jungle. Divide into groups. The boats can take no more than ten people at a time. The mothers and small children will go first. My family will go last."

For the first time since we left our village, I saw hope on some people's faces. Yet most of us were still frightened.

My father sensed the fear in our group as well. He led us in prayer, then said, "All right, the first group needs to head out."

I think it must have been about nine o'clock at night. We hadn't had anything to eat in almost two days.

The first two groups piled into the boats. No sooner had the last person climbed aboard than the boats took off across the river. They meandered along, doing their best to look like a couple of fishing boats working the river.

Sitting on the bank and waiting for our family's turn to come, I heard the gunfire filling the air and watched the tracer bullets flying from both sides of the Mekong. As the night grew darker, I heard the distinctive *whoosh* of mortar fire followed by an explosion on the opposite side of the river. From time to time, the shells fell short and exploded in the river.

Yet the worst sounds of the night, the ones that haunt me in my nightmares, were the wails echoing along the river. "Save me! I'm drowning!" Off in the distance, a mother crying out, "Save my child."

The voices never stopped from the moment the sun went down until it came up again. The cries, so desperate, so filled with pain, came from those with no choice but to try to cross the Mekong without a boat.

Most of these people didn't make it. Those who didn't drown were shot by the Pathet Lao. So many people died in that river, especially children. Oh, so many of my people.

When I close my eyes, I hear the cries.

About an hour after they'd first set out, the boats returned to pick up the next two groups. They ferried people across the river through the night until my family, along with three of my uncles, were the only ones left on the Lao side of the Mekong. By the time we climbed into the boats, the eastern sky was starting to light up.

I didn't realize how small the boats really were until ten of us crammed into this little fishing boat built for no more than two. With so many people, the boat floated low in the water and the slightest wave splashed over the side, soaking us all. I thought for sure we would sink.

Our boat had barely set out from shore when the driver said to my father, "I don't think we can do this right now. It will be light before we get to the other side. We'll be shot."

"So what are we supposed to do?" my father asked. "We can't go back and press our luck staying where we did yesterday."

"I know of an island in the river where you should be safe. Lots of brush. No one ever goes there."

"Whatever you think is best."

Another night had passed, and still we had no food, no water. Nothing.

The boat owners hid their vessels in the reeds off the shore of the island. Around noon, they came to my father and said, "We're hungry. There's no sense in hiding here on this island with you all day. Without you in our boats, the soldiers won't bother us. We're going back to Laos to get something to eat. Once the sun sets, we'll come back and take you the rest of the way to Thailand."

"I know you must be hungry," my father said, which to me was the understatement of the year; our last real meal had come the night before we'd left Num Chang, which felt like a week ago. "But I prefer that you stay. If you must go, please leave one of the boats here, just in case something happens to you. Otherwise, we'll be stranded."

"Nothing will happen to us. Listen, we're hungry, and we're taking our boats to get some food."

"Please take only one boat."

"Stop telling us what to do with our boats." I could tell the man was getting angry with my father. He was already mad that my father hadn't paid the entire price in advance for ferrying us across the river.

"I'm not trying to tell you how to run your business, but we are vulnerable here. We can't stay on this island, and you're our only way to the other side."

The driver cursed. "We're leaving, and there's nothing you can do to stop us."

My father looked at my mother. "Now."

She reached under her dress and pulled out a .38 my father had strapped to her leg before we'd left our village almost a month earlier.

I couldn't believe my eyes, and neither could the boat owners.

My father pointed the pistol at the two men. "This is the way it's going to be. One of you can get some food, but the other isn't going anywhere. Do you understand me? I gave you your chance. I tried to be reasonable, but you gave me no choice. Now you'll do things my way."

The two men cursed at my father, but he was correct. They had no choice but to do things his way.

Still, they did a cruel thing. One of the men went to Laos and bought a bag of grilled chicken and sticky rice and brought it back to the island. Then he and the other man sat and ate every bite in front of all of us without offering even one of the smallest children a grain of rice.

My empty stomach ached; my mouth watered. I would've given anything for just one bite.

The sun had barely set when one of the two boat owners yelled at my father. "It's time. Get in the boat. Let's go."

"No, it isn't dark enough." My father refused to yield to their anger.

Finally, night came and with it the cries from the river. We climbed back into the boats and took off. At one point, I saw an empty inner tube and knew someone hadn't made it.

The moment our boat touched the shore, the drivers cursed at my family. "Get *out.*" Throwing our few possessions onto the ground and pushing the women and children out like baggage, they said, "Give us our money."

My father handed them every valuable we had. Other family members were supposed to help pay for our passage, but when the time came, they claimed they didn't have the money.

The two boat owners snatched up the treasures, jumped in their boats, and off they went toward Laos.

About the time the boats took off, we heard someone running through the brush toward us. Lots of someones.

A squad of soldiers burst out, guns drawn.

I thought for sure we'd been caught by the Pathet Lao and NVA. As the children in our group burst into tears, I looked for a place to hide.

The soldiers shouted something I didn't understand.

My father answered in a language other than Hmong or Lao. Then he turned to my family. "It's okay. They're Thai soldiers."

At long last, we were safe.

12

"I Actually Belong Here"

"It looks like I may be here a while, little brother," I said to Kham Dy from my hotel room in downtown Las Vegas during one of our daily calls during the World Series of Poker. While I would have loved to chat with him in person, at this point in the tournament, being by myself was probably best.

"How long is a while?" Kham asked.

"I don't play again for a couple of days. There are still too many players to get everyone into the Amazon Room all at once, so I'm guaranteed at least one more day. I believe I can do better than that. My chip count is in the top 20 percent of the field."

"Are you kidding me? Brother, that is very impressive."

"Thank you. Not to sound overly confident, but I honestly think I can finish in the money."

"What's the least you will take home if you cash out?"

"Over $20,000."

"Wow. And how much did it cost you to play in the tournament where you won your seat?"

"Two twenty-five."

My brother laughed. "So when do you plan on telling Father?"

"I wish I could call him and tell him right now."

"You aren't going to, are you?"

"No. But if I make it into the 621 who cash out, I'll try to get him to Vegas to watch. I could use his support."

My brother laughed again. "Good luck with that, big brother. I think you have a better chance of winning the whole thing than of getting Father to come to Las Vegas to watch one of his sons in the world's largest poker tournament. You know how he feels about cards and gambling."

"Why do you think I never told him I took up poker?"

Kham Dy and I had talked about this before. Even though he is a pastor, Kham Dy never questioned my decision to take up poker. He didn't like gambling any more than my father or wife did, but he also understood I never spent more of our family's money on poker than many of the men in his church spent on golf every weekend.

"So what can I do to help you, Brother?" Kham Dy asked.

"Just pray. Pray I'll have the patience, discipline, and wisdom I need to play my best. I want to represent Jesus the best I can while I'm here. Pray I will."

"Of course."

We spent some time praying before hanging up.

After all that the two of us had been through together, I

couldn't imagine facing this challenge without him on my side.

Some people think poker and God are contradictory. I get this from both sides of the question. During my run at the 2007 World Series of Poker, several people criticized me for praying at the table. To them, God didn't have a place in poker. Some church people have criticized me because like my father, they believe cards and poker have no place in the life of a Christian.

I had to wrestle with this myself before I took up the game. Could a religious person play poker without losing all credibility? To me, the answer was easy. I found myself attracted to poker for the mental challenge it presents. Luck plays a part, but the real game comes down to who can best apply and withstand the pressure each hand potentially brings. When I started playing, I didn't take food out of my children's mouths or use the mortgage money to try to strike it rich. While I played to win, I never risked money I couldn't afford to lose. I never expected to recoup the $50 per week I'd set aside when I first started playing the game. Essentially, it was money I spent on a hobby, which happened to be poker. I see this as no more of an ethical dilemma than a tennis player faces when deciding whether to join the local tennis club.

Other players as well as some commentators criticized me for bringing God so openly to the poker table. Some saw my praying as an attempt to get God to change my luck or make the cards fall my way. I can see why some players didn't welcome this. Going up against another player and the luck of the draw is difficult enough without having to take on the

Almighty as well.

To me, though, praying at the poker table is not a good luck ritual. I pray because prayer and God are a large part of who I am.

As I've mentioned, I grew up in a Christian family, although that was not always the case for the Yangs. My grandfather grew up worshipping the traditional Hmong gods and spirits. When he was a boy, he had a dream about a man in a black robe pointing at him and saying, "I have great things I want you to do for me."

When my grandfather awoke, he went to his father and told him about his dream. "What does this mean, Father?"

His father was excited. "This is a sign. A sign that has stood for many, many generations. You have been chosen to become a shaman. The spirits have vested you with a special power, and now you must use it."

In the traditional animist Hmong religious culture, the shaman is the highest, most respected member of the community. He communes with the spirits for the people of the village as a healer, spiritual guide, and community leader. To have a son become a shaman is one of the highest honors any family could have.

The presence of a shaman in the family also meant they would never go hungry. Whenever someone gives an offering to one of the gods, a portion of their sacrifice goes to the shaman himself. If you're told to sacrifice your prize bull, you do it. The shaman eats the meat not burned up on the altar. In a country where hunger abounds, becoming a shaman was like winning the lottery.

My grandfather went away and trained with an elder shaman. There he learned all of the traditional rituals and ceremonies as well as how to discern the signs of nature. One of his most important roles was that of healer. When a person became ill, my people believed the person's spirit moved away from the body. If it moved far enough away, the person would die. The shaman could bring the spirit back only if he determined that the family and friends had presented the right offerings and sacrifices. Even though most Hmong in Laos were very poor, they did whatever the shaman commanded and paid any price. If they had only one cow and the shaman told them to sacrifice it and give the meat to him, that's exactly what they did. He always had the ultimate word.

For twenty or thirty years, my grandfather led his village as the chief spiritual leader. No one commanded more respect.

Then one day my grandfather became extremely ill himself. While fighting a high fever through the night, he had another dream. This time, a man in a glorious white robe told him, "You must leave everything behind and come, follow Me. I have a new mission for you."

My grandfather awoke in a fright. He had no interest in changing anything about his life. He was the single most powerful figure in his village. To turn his back on the role of shaman and the wealth it brought to his family, to say nothing of the beliefs handed down to him from generation to generation, was unthinkable, but he couldn't shake the image of the man.

As time went by, my grandfather's illness grew worse. Finally, he told my grandmother about his dream. Word spread from her to people from a nearby village who happened to be Christians.

A couple traveled to my grandfather's village and went into his home, where he lay sick. One of the men looked at him, pointed, and said, "The man in white you saw in your dream was Jesus. He wants you to leave the ways of shamanism and follow Him. You will then bring many people into a true knowledge of God."

The man might as well have told my grandfather to throw all his possessions into a pile and set them on fire. "I can't do that. I'll be driven out of my village. Everyone will mock me, and my family will starve."

As time passed and he grew weaker, though, he finally decided he couldn't ignore the dream any longer. *I'm going to die anyway. I might as well give this so-called Savior, Jesus, a try.*

Believe it or not, my grandfather quickly began to get better. Before long, every symptom disappeared, making a true believer out of him. Having always thought of himself as a great and powerful shaman, he now understood Jesus was much greater and more powerful than he.

Just as he had feared, however, my grandfather was driven out of his village. People shunned the entire family, including my father, who was a teenager at the time. Critics said, "You've betrayed your people by going along with this white man's religion."

Undeterred, my grandfather knew Jesus was real and that neither he nor his entire family would turn back from following Him. Until the day he died, my grandfather firmly believed God had a mission for him, and he did his best to live it every day.

My grandfather passed this conviction on to my father, who passed it on to me.

Now, in everything I do, I want God to use me in some way. This is what I'd meant back in 2005 when I'd pointed at the ESPN broadcast of the World Series of Poker and declared to my wife that I would use anything I won for good. If God were to bless me with success at the biggest tournament I could ever hope to play, He would surely have something bigger in mind than simply giving Jerry Yang some prize money.

After my first day of play, I felt this conviction more than ever. Sitting alone in the smelly hotel room after hanging up with my brother, I began to seriously ponder the possibility of cashing out. Even if I finished in six hundred twenty-first place, the $20,000 would change my family's life. The thought excited me but also filled me with a great sense of responsibility. I knew I needed to use whatever I won wisely, to seek God's plan for the money and my life.

That's why I prayed so much at the poker table.

Believe me when I say the praying you might have seen me do on the ESPN broadcast of the tournament was minimal compared to the amount I did back at my hotel. You would have prayed, too, walking through this neighborhood.

During my days off, I went back to the Rio, camera in hand, and did all the touristy things, collecting more autographs and taking my picture with the celebrities who were milling around. A lot of famous actors play poker. I even met

Spider-Man, Tobey Maguire, which thrilled me.

Every time I went back to the Rio, I entered the Amazon Room and watched, always leaving feeling more determined to do well, more focused on my game, and ready to get back to the table to see where this ride might take me. I'd come to Vegas to have fun. Now, with almost 100,000 in chips, I had to get much more serious.

Back at my hotel, I pulled out some of the notes I'd made both during the first round and prior to coming to Las Vegas. After I won my seat in the main event, I went back over the televised poker tournaments I'd recorded and made careful notes on how each pro played. I wanted to be prepared if I found myself at the table with one of them. I also reviewed strategy in the poker books I'd read and reread many times. The caliber of play from this point forward would improve dramatically, and I didn't want to get pulled into rookie mistakes.

In poker, as in any sport, if you're more prepared than your opponents, you stand a better chance of winning. If I lost, it would not be for lack of planning.

I survived my second day of play. Actually, I did more than survive. My chip stack put me in the top 25 percent of those still alive.

From this point forward, I would play every day. Now I could settle into a routine. Each evening, I drove up Interstate 15 from the Rio to my hotel. The fifteen minutes in the car gave me a chance to decompress, and the walk from my car to the hotel gave me a chance and a reason to pray. Thank God I was never mugged.

Once I was back in my room, I went through my same preparation. I called my wife, then watched a little television to decompress. Early the next morning I got up, took a cold fifteen-minute shower, prayed, read my Bible, and meditated. I even did some stretching and basic exercises. At 11:30, my brother called and the two of us prayed together. By the time play resumed at noon, I was focused and ready to go.

About this time, I had an epiphany. As I went through my routine, it slowly dawned on me that this room in this hotel was a huge blessing. With its mildew creeping up the bathroom tiles and its roaches scattering whenever I turned on the light and the crime on the street outside my window, this setting was not so different from the one I'd grown up in.

This place kept me grounded in who I was. Even as my chip stack grew, coming back to my downtown hotel kept me from thinking too highly of myself.

It also helped me stay focused on the task at hand. If I'd stayed in a nice hotel on the Strip, I might have been swept away by the glitz and glamour of Las Vegas and lost sight of why I was here. After my playing day ended, I might well have gone to the shows. Instead, when I got to my hotel, I stayed in my room until it was time to resume play.

When I'd first seen my downtown hotel, it had been the last place I'd wanted to spend the next twelve days. Yet as I climbed the ranks during the tournament, I realized this was the perfect place for me.

When play began on day three, excitement filled the Amazon

Room. The veterans called this money day. Everyone still alive at the end of the day would cash out.

I knew the minimum payout amount by heart. I'd written it on a slip of paper and kept it in my pocket while I played. During breaks, I stared at it. *All I have to do is finish in the top 621, and I take home $20,230.*

I didn't let myself think about it, but I was also well aware that whoever finished at number 622 took home nothing.

This day I felt confident going in. Given the size of my chip stack, I knew I could cash out, unless of course I had a complete breakdown. And I was not going to allow myself to be drawn into that position.

I sensed fear in those with short stacks. In poker, fear plants a target on a player's forehead, and I took aim. The closer I got to the money, the more aggressively I played.

Aggression doesn't mean recklessness. Those on the bubble, those who needed a miracle to climb into the money, played recklessly. They had no choice but to take one chance after another and play hands they normally would've folded away. I took advantage of their desperation and pushed them as hard as I could.

By 5:00 in the evening, we were down to 650 players.

I could feel it. Everyone, especially the short stacks at every table, could feel it. No one wanted to bust out before the bubble boy, the last player to bust before cashing out. I wasn't worried about it. I knew I was about to surpass my wildest dreams.

Then, during a hand, a floor man started applauding loudly in the middle of the room. "Congratulations, everyone!"

The place went nuts. It was bubble party time. The players

at my table jumped up, slapped one another on the back, and high-fived.

As soon as all the hands were played, the round ended and cell phones popped out everywhere.

I immediately called my wife. "Guess what, Mommy," I nearly yelled into the phone. "I did it! I'm in the money."

I felt as if I'd just climbed a huge mountain. I had already won. Now I knew I couldn't lose.

After hanging up, I made another call. One I'd wanted to make for a long time.

Yet one I never wanted to make.

I took a deep breath, then punched in the number. My little brother Reagan answered. After briefly telling him what had happened, I said, "Please put Father on the line."

After a pause I heard, "*Nyob zoo*," which is Hmong for "hello."

"Father," I said, also in Hmong.

"Vaam," my father said, "it is so good to hear from you. How are you?"

"I'm doing well, Father. In fact . . ." I hesitated, afraid to tell him where I was because I knew how he felt about cards and gambling.

"What is it, Vaam?"

"Father, I'm in Las Vegas for the World Series of Poker. I am doing very well. So well, in fact, that even if I lost right now, I'd take home at least $20,000. But I'm not in danger of losing right now. I stand a very good chance of being one of the top finishers."

He didn't say a word, but I didn't give him a chance. "Father, I would like you to come to Las Vegas to be with me while I play these last couple of days. I really need your support."

The next thing I heard was my brother's voice. "Father handed me the phone and walked away. What did you say to him?"

"He now knows his son is a poker player."

"Give him time, Vaam. Give him time."

We talked for a short while, and he prayed with me, as he did every time we talked. Then he said, "Don't let Father's reaction get to you or distract you. You keep playing the way you have been, big brother. I'm very proud of you, and Father will be as well. You can do this. I know you can."

"Thank you, Brother."

As disappointed as I was with my father's reaction, I realized my brother was right. I could do this. I knew it.

13

An Improbable Climb

Entering day four of the main event, I could feel the excitement. The 700,000 chips in my stack put me in a strong position among the 337 players left in the tournament. Even if I foolishly went all in and lost the first hand of the day—something I would never, ever do—I would go home with nearly $40,000. If I survived the day, that amount would increase to almost $60,000. The longer I lasted, the more my confidence soared. I was having the tournament of my life.

But then Texas Hold 'Em did what it always seems to do.

Unlike day one, when I'd drawn pocket aces seven times in two hours, I couldn't draw a hand this day to save my life. Or if I did, something would go awry. Another player always seemed to hit a miracle card on the river and beat me. In poker, when a strong hand is beaten by a long-shot hand, we call it a bad beat.

It's one thing to have pocket kings and lose to someone

holding ace-queen who draws an ace on the river. But it's another thing entirely to have pocket aces and lose to someone playing seven-two off suit who draws a miracle straight to take the pot. Those losses stick with you.

Day four was my day of bad beats and bad hands. I won a few pots, but just about the time I regained my confidence, I lost several in a row.

About halfway through the day, my chip stack had shrunk from 700,000 to 300,000. *Patience, Jerry, patience,* I warned myself, but sometimes I have trouble taking my own advice.

After the cards were dealt, I watched my eight opponents closely. The first one or two folded.

Then Maria Ho, one of the few women still alive in the tournament at this point, raised.

I studied her, looking for any sign of bluffing.

The next person called.

Now it was my turn to act. Only then did I look at my cards. Ace-three. The combination had an 8 percent chance of winning a pot. Smart poker strategy says to fold and wait for better cards. A focused, disciplined, patient player almost always does exactly that.

But I wasn't thinking about patience or focus or smart poker strategy. I kept staring at a stack of chips that a few hours earlier had been twice as large, and I wanted to do something to get the chips back. *Now.*

"I'm all in." I said it with the same amount of emotion I might use to announce that the paint on the side of the house has dried.

"I fold," Maria Ho said.

Good. That had been my plan exactly. I'd wanted all the other players at the table to think I had a very large pair and send them running for cover. The last thing I wanted to do was risk busting out on the flop, turn, or river and have to go home.

"I call," the other player said.

Noooooo, that's not what you're supposed to do. Even though I was yelling in my mind, I acted as if I'd wanted him to call all along.

I turned my cards, revealing the ace-three.

My opponent smiled. He held pocket eights. Pocket eights have a 57 percent chance of winning a hand as compared to my ace-three's puny odds.

"Good call," I said.

I stood, said a quick prayer, and waited for the flop. The cards hit the table. King, seven, four. No aces but also no eights.

The four gave me an outside chance for a straight—a *very* outside chance. To make it, I needed a two or a five on the turn, then the opposite on the river. The odds of that happening were slim to none.

The dealer burned a card, then dealt the turn card: a five. I still had a chance for a gut shot straight. Now I just needed a two on the river. My only other chance of winning was for the river card to hit an ace. My tournament now came down to neither skill nor discipline but to luck. Pure, dumb luck.

The dealer burned another card, then turned over the river.

I could hardly believe my eyes. There staring up at me was the most beautiful two of hearts I had seen in my life. On my day of bad beats, I gave another player one myself. I let out a huge sigh of relief.

"Congratulations, Jerry," the player graciously said as he shook my hand.

That miracle gut shot straight turned my up-and-down day around. By the time I sealed my chips into a bag for the night and headed back to my smelly hotel room, I was up to 1.15 million in chips.

The tournament chip leader, Dag Martin Mikkelsen, held a three-to-one lead over me with 3.7 million. That didn't matter. I was closing in on ninth place, and that's where I needed to be at the end of day six to make the final table. Once you make it there, anything can happen.

Yet I still had to survive two long days.

Day five lasted fourteen hours. Play began at noon with 112 players. We didn't stop until after two the following morning, when the thirty-seventh place finisher finally busted out.

Day four had frustrated me with all its bad beats, but day five gave me a little break. I still had to play smart, disciplined poker, but I made enough hands to stay out of danger. Though the prize money increases with each round, that doesn't keep players on the brink of busting out from playing erratically. Thankfully, I managed to keep myself from getting damaged by any of them.

I also managed to stay relatively invisible. From the start on day one, no one had penciled Jerry Yang into their list of most dangerous players, which had allowed me to fly under the radar.

By this day, the players with healthy chip stacks had locked into survival mode, while those with dwindling stacks kicked into desperation gear. Neither type paid a lot of attention to a praying psychologist from Temecula, California.

My most dramatic moment of the day didn't come at the poker table but during one of the breaks.

The longer I survived, the more I wanted my father there. Though I had a master's degree in psychology and had completed all of the coursework for my PhD, my father still sometimes saw me as that mischievous little Tom Sawyer who invaded the henhouse with his buddies. By bringing him to the World Series of Poker, I could show him I'd become the man he'd always hoped I'd be: disciplined, focused, able to meet even my loftiest goals.

"Hello, Father," I said to him over the phone.

"Yes, Vaam," he said flatly. I could tell he was still disappointed with me for being in Sin City playing the devil's game.

"Father, I would like you to be with me while I play in the World Series of Poker. Before you say no, I want to tell you, Father, that I'm doing very well. I'm currently assured of making it to the next round of thirty-six, which means I'll take home at least $285,000."

"I don't see how that's possible. For five generations, we Yangs have known that no one can gamble their way to riches. Only a fool gambles away what they worked so hard to earn. You, of all my sons, should know this. You're much too intelligent to do something so foolish."

"I can assure you, dear Father, that not only is it possible but it is indeed happening right now. Kham Dy and I talk every day. He knows I speak the truth. If you doubt me, he can take you to the World Series website and show you that what I say is true."

"And how much did you gamble away to try to win all of this money? The stakes must be very high if they're giving so much to the winners."

"I didn't risk any of my family's money. You taught me too well to do something so foolish. No, I entered a tournament with money I'd won. Father, I spent merely $225 to get to where I am now. I'm a businessman, and I believe that's a very good return on my money. Wouldn't you agree?"

My father said little—that is, until my brother showed him my name on the computer screen and my place at that moment in the main event. I wasn't there to see it, but my brother said my father's jaw dropped.

"Okay, Vaam, okay. I believe you."

"Does that mean you'll come to Las Vegas and watch me the rest of the tournament? I very much need your support and wisdom."

For a long time, I heard nothing but silence on the other end of the line. Finally, my father spoke up. "Yes, Vaam, I will get there as soon as I can."

I made arrangements with my brother-in-law to buy airplane tickets for both my mother and father. I picked them up at the airport before heading back to the Rio. Although

I would stay at my downtown hotel, I reserved a suite for my parents at the Rio. If all went according to plan, I and my entire family would join them there.

For that to happen, I had to survive one long, hazardous day.

14

Next Stop: The Final Table

I may have flown under the radar on day five of the World Series of Poker, but there was no chance of that happening on day six. Every one of the thirty-six players who started the day, especially the few remaining amateurs like me, wore a huge target. And with just over 5 million in chips, on a day when play began with an average stack of 4 million, I definitely had a bull's-eye plastered on me.

Early in my poker career, I had discovered that rookies play erratically, amateurs play the cards, and pros play the other players. Very good players, like all of the thirty-six remaining, look for any advantage they can find, even if they have to create it themselves. As one of the least experienced players, I knew everyone else was looking to take advantage of me.

I was in the sixth position at the feature table, the one set up specifically for ESPN's television audience and where the final nine would ultimately play. At all the other tables, spectators stood outside ropes; around the feature table, they sat in grandstands.

The sixth position placed me in the middle of one of the long sides of the table. I prefer sitting on the end, where I can watch everyone else simply by looking up. In the sixth position, I had to look from side to side to follow the action.

An hour and a half went by, and I held my own. Then I found myself seated between two professional poker players, Daniel Alaei and Kenny Tran. Alaei was in the small blind, and I was in the big blind, which at that time were 30,000 and 60,000 in chips.

The action started with Kenny Tran, who was seated to my immediate left. He folded.

Tuan Lam followed by folding, as did Jason Koshi, chip leader Lee Childs, John Kalmar, and Stefan Mattsson.

Daniel Alaei looked at his cards. "I call." Since he was in the small blind, he had to put only another 30,000 into the pot to stay in the hand. This is called limping in. If he'd had a strong hand, he would have raised.

Now it was my turn to act. I looked at my cards. Ace-ten. I didn't have to raise to stay in. I could simply check and essentially see the flop for free, since, as the big blind, I had 60,000 in the pot whether I played the hand or not.

However, I sensed weakness in Alaei. His limping in from the small blind told me he had a borderline hand at best. If I projected strength, I might force him to fold.

Here's where table position came into the equation. If I'd been in Kenny Tran's seat, I wouldn't have played ace-ten. But as the last person to act on a hand in which everyone had folded except the small blind, who limped in, I felt I had a strong enough hand to take down the pot.

"I raise, 260,000." With the blinds and the antes, the pot was already up to 200,000. By raising over the pot size, I was in effect telling Alaei I had a very good hand and was not afraid to play it. His chip stack was one-third the size of mine, and I planned to bully him with it if I could.

"I'm all in," he replied.

That surprised me. I stood and stared at his chip stack. Now I faced a tough decision. With my chip lead, calling didn't place my tournament in danger, but I hate to double up anyone, especially a pro. Giving a pro chips is like waving a red flag in front of a bull.

Think this through, Jerry, I told myself. *What do you see in front of you? He may well have a pocket pair and was just trying to draw you in with that weak call.* I pondered that for a moment. *No, I don't think so. That's not the way I've seen him play on television. This is the kind of play he makes with a hand like ace-five or maybe a small pair, like threes or fours. He's a tight player. He never limps in and turns around and goes all in. I think he's trying to steal this pot and build up his chip stack. He wants you to fold.*

"Call," I finally said.

Daniel stood and turned his cards at the same time I turned mine. His ace-five didn't surprise me at all.

While we both had aces, my ten gave me a huge advantage, unless, of course, some funny cards turned over on the flop, like a two, three, and four, giving him a straight.

Stranger things have happened.

No sooner had I stood up than Kenny Tran jumped up like he had a stake in the pot. "I had ace-ten as well." He said this to Daniel Alaei, not me, as if I didn't belong at the table with a couple of pros like him and Daniel.

For a player to stand and talk through the rest of the hand after folding is unusual. Most sit back and watch. I've even dozed off a time or two. The one thing they never do is talk, especially trash talk. I guess there's always one exception to every rule.

This was part of Kenny's game. He didn't mean anything personal by it. He was simply trying to crawl inside my head. Whether I won or lost, he knew he would come up against me in a future hand and wanted to push me on tilt long before that happened.

Daniel knew I had him on the ropes. We waited for the flop to fall. "Come on, nothing funny," I said as the cards were dealt.

"Nothing funny?" Kenny Tran said.

I didn't respond.

The flop came down. Three-seven-queen. The three gave Alaei a remote chance of a straight. I would have said it was an impossible chance if I hadn't hit one like it myself two days before.

Then came the turn. An eight. Only a five on the river could beat me now.

"Nothing funny," I said in almost a whisper.

"'Nothing funny,' he said." Kenny Tran leaned in and looked at me. "What's funny? Which card do you think is funny?"

A couple players laughed.

I ignored him completely, then whispered a small prayer. Something like, "Help me, Jesus."

"Yo." Kenny Tran waved at me. "You cannot pray on the table."

I shot Kenny a look, which was the wrong thing to do. He really was starting to get to me.

He shook his head. "No, you can't do it."

"And now we will see the river card," the announcer said.

Just then Kenny Tran pointed at the table with a theatric gesture. "Five!"

The river card *was* a five. I lost the hand and doubled up Daniel Alaei. Worse yet, I nearly lost my cool. Kenny Tran was doing his best to put me on tilt, and he nearly succeeded.

Okay, Jerry, don't let him get to you. I turned around and caught sight of my father sitting in the stands. I thought about all the times I'd watched men try to intimidate and manipulate him. But he'd never given in. No matter how high the stakes, my father always kept his cool. To go any further, I would have to do the same.

I regained my composure, but now I had to regain my chips. If I hadn't known it before, I now knew this was going to be the biggest test of my adult life. After losing that hand to Daniel Alaei, I found myself down to 3 million in chips. At that rate, I would bust out in just over an hour.

I kept fighting. Within another hour or two, I got my stack up to 8 million. I could breathe again.

I shouldn't have exhaled, because before I knew it, I'd dropped 2 million. Then I was back down to 3 million.

I felt as if I'd stepped onto Space Mountain at Disneyland. This was not a good day. I wished my parents had come a couple days before, when I'd actually been playing well.

Yet no matter how up and down my day was, I was still alive. I didn't need to take the chip lead; I just needed to hold on a little while longer.

About an hour after the bad beat to Daniel Alaei, I bluffed Lee Childs, the chip leader, into folding pocket kings to me. On that hand, an ace hit the table on the flop, which made him think I had a pair of aces. As soon as the ace hit, I bet a million in chips, which nearly doubled the pot. His fold gave me a nice boost and made me hungry for more.

A few hands later, Lee Childs and I went back up against one another. He had middle position, which meant four players acted before him and three after. All those before him folded. When it came time for Lee to act, he looked at his cards, waited, then said, "Raise," as he tossed 240,000 chips into the pot. With a big blind of 60,000, his raise came to 180,000. At three times the big blind, it was an aggressive raise.

Stefan Mattsson was the next to act. Without a word, he tossed 240,000 into the pot to call.

Now it was my turn. It had felt so good to say, "One million," the last time I'd raised Childs that I thought I'd do it again. More than that, I knew I'd bullied him into folding pocket kings the last time I'd raised a million. No matter what he had, short of pocket aces, I thought I could get him to fold one more time.

I stood, grabbed my chips, and said, "One million."

Kenny Tran was the next to act. He flipped some chips around for a while, then tossed in his hand.

The action went back to Lee Childs, who rested his chin on his hands, looked at me, and said, "Why so much, Jerry?"

I didn't respond.

Childs stared at the chips on the table for what felt like a very long time. Though I wanted to hear him say, "I fold," instead he slid a million in chips to the middle.

The action came back around to Mattsson, who immediately folded.

Once again, it was just Lee Childs and me. The flop came: nine of clubs, four of hearts, three of clubs.

I was the first to act. I stood and said, "Two million."

That sent Childs to his feet. He yanked off his sunglasses and let out a long sigh. After what felt like a long time once again, he said, "I don't think I can lay it down." He paused again, took a deep breath, and said, "I'm all in."

People in the stands yelled as if Childs had just scored the winning touchdown in the Super Bowl.

It was not what I'd wanted Childs to say. His line was supposed to be, "I fold." I wanted him to think I had a very large pocket pair. In truth, I had nothing but an ace-seven, a very weak hand. Now I faced a difficult decision.

Childs pushed in 5 million in chips. It would cost me 3 million to raise, and I didn't have 3 million left. I was down to

2.5 million. Yet, at the same time, I already had over 3 million invested in the pot. How could I let it go without a fight?

I stood and stared at the flop. My pride wanted to call. Patience and discipline demanded that I swallow my pride and utter the two little words I didn't want to say.

Okay, I *couldn't* bring myself to say them. I slid my cards to the dealer and folded.

Oh, that hurt.

The only way to survive a marathon like the main event is to fold when you know you're beaten rather than pouring chips into the pot just to see what the other guy may have. Losing so many chips hurt, but losing that hand and busting out completely would have hurt much more.

The roller coaster ride took a turn a few hours later. Eventually I climbed up to number five on the leader board with 8.5 million in chips, which was well within the top nine who made the final table. A few hours later, I dropped to 1.8 million and found myself in serious danger of busting out. I knew I had to play disciplined poker, not letting my emotions get the best of me.

Over the next two hours, I waited for both cards and position. Several times when I found myself on the button—that is, being the last one to act in a hand before the blinds—I went all in. On the surface, these were aggressive moves, but I didn't fall into the trap of blind aggression. I went all in only when those with large stacks had already folded. Someone with a stack of over 10 million wouldn't think twice of calling my puny 2 million if it meant potentially eliminating one more rival for a seat at the final table.

No, when I went all in from the button, I tried to make sure anyone tempted to call had to put their tournament on the line to do so. By going all in prior to the flop, I took chance and luck out of the equation. Thankfully my strategy worked and they always folded, leaving me to pick up the blinds and antes. By this point, the big blind had climbed to over half a million. Winning three or four of those added up to a nice stack.

Slowly but surely, I built up my chip stack and stayed in the game. All I wanted to do was survive till the final table. No one ever won the World Series of Poker on day six, yet all but nine players would lose.

Midnight came. I thought my mother might go up to her room to sleep, but she and my father stayed behind the rope, watching everything I did. They didn't understand the game, but that didn't matter. Just having them there meant the world to me. My chip stack looked pathetic compared to the leaders'. I had 2.5 million; the top five averaged 16.4 million. I didn't care about the top five, just the top nine. As long as I was alive, I had a shot.

Once again, I found myself on the button. Everyone was folding on the way around the table to me. I looked at my cards: pocket eights. The clock in my head counted down: *four . . . three . . . two . . . one . . .* "I'm all in."

The small blind folded.

Alex Kravchenko sat in the big blind. He thought for a minute or so, then said, "I call."

I shook my head and prepared for the worst. He turned a king-queen of diamonds.

My eights won, and I doubled up.

Kravchenko took my place on the short stack for the tournament with 1.3 million.

Unfortunately, before I could even enjoy the elation of winning that hand, two hands later, he turned the tables and went all in on me after I'd raised half a million.

I called with my king-nine of clubs.

He showed pocket tens, and I ended up doubling him up.

Most of the night, the two of us had almost the same amount in chips, which wasn't saying much. Neither of us looked like contenders to last until day seven.

Another hour had passed. Out of the thirty-six players who started day six, eleven were still alive. Kenny Tran, the player who'd tried to throw me off my game twelve hours before, was not one of the eleven. He busted out at 9:30, finishing in sixteenth place. A funny card on the river knocked him out, a lowly two of clubs.

As play continued at one in the morning, I found myself in eleventh place. Dead last.

The good news was that even if I went out on the next hand, I would take home almost half a million dollars, but I refused to let myself think like that. I didn't care how much I would win if I busted out. I had one goal, and that was to claw my way up two more spots to the top nine.

The blinds had climbed to a level where I couldn't be as

patient as I might have liked. Each cycle through the small and big blinds left me a million in chips poorer and that much closer to elimination.

Unfortunately, I couldn't bluff my way up those two spots. Everyone always calls the bluffs of the short stack.

Over the past several hours, I had so frequently gone all in to take the blinds and antes that I'd lost count. It was the only thing keeping me in the tournament. I won a few other hands, but the longer play continued, my day turned more down than up. Such is life on the short stack.

The cards were dealt. I sat on the button, last to act before the blinds. Only six players remained at my table. The first two to act folded to me.

I looked at my cards. Pocket eights. A good hand but definitely not a great one. I glanced at my short stack. I had no choice. "I'm all in."

The small blind folded, which was exactly what I'd wanted.

Alex Kravchenko, who'd bounced around the bottom of the chip pile with me all day long, was the next to act. He'd hit a pretty good roll of late and had a decent chip stack but not one large enough to take the risk of calling, unless of course he had a very good hand.

"I call," Kravchenko said.

Nuts. Not what I'd wanted to hear. *Okay, Jerry, you can survive this.*

Then Alex flipped his cards. King-queen of diamonds, a very dangerous hand. Out of the 169 possible hands in Texas Hold 'Em, king-queen same suit is the twelfth best pocket hand. Pocket eights is the thirteenth.

I turned my cards.

Alex looked at me, smiled slightly, and said, "I didn't expect you to have a hand. I thought you were trying to steal one."

A little earlier, I'd played a queen-three and actually hit a queen to win the hand. He thought I was playing something just as weak this time.

I didn't say anything, or if I did I was too nervous to remember.

Unlike me, Alex had a large enough stack to cover me and keep playing if he lost the hand. Furthermore, he had several ways of making a hand, and five cards were left to make it with.

I had to dodge a lot of bullets to stay alive. Out of the forty-two cards left in the deck, thirty-three would help him, and only two would help me.

"Lord, let me survive this hand," I prayed. "Just let me survive this hand. I cannot get busted out now. I need to go on." Inside, I also prayed, *Oh, God, if I lose, please give me the strength to go out with grace and dignity.*

The flop came. Nine-six-six, one of which was a diamond. I was still alive. To make the flush, he had to hit diamonds on both the turn and the river. For the straight, he had to hit a jack and a ten. Of course, if another king or queen showed up, I was dead.

The turn hit the table. Ten of clubs. No chance for a flush, but now any face card on the river would send me and my parents back to California. There were potentially ten face cards still looming in the deck. Ten out of thirty-nine.

I prayed harder.

The river came: a nothing card.

I took the pot and doubled my stack. More importantly, I survived.

Ten minutes later at the other table, the 1998 main event champion, Scotty Nguyen, busted out. He made a farewell speech to the crowd, but I didn't pay much attention. I had now officially made the top ten.

After a twenty-minute break, play would resume at the not-quite-final table. The ten remaining players would all take our seats at the feature table, where we would play until one player busted out. At that moment, play would stop until noon the following day. That's when the real final table would begin.

It was 2:00 a.m. on the dot. We'd been playing poker for fourteen straight hours. I heard more yawns than cheers from the spectators in the stands. I didn't dare take off my dark glasses. I knew my eyes were red, with dark circles underneath. We'd played until two in the morning on day five, which meant all of us had begun day six more than a little sleep deprived. I'd climbed out of bed earlier than usual to pick up my parents at the airport. I don't think they had any idea what they were getting themselves into.

Play began again. I was in seat four. Thanks to Alex Kravchenko doubling me up, my chip stack was now up to 6 million, good enough for seventh place. All I had to do was finish in the top nine to live to play another day. Alex wasn't quite so lucky. He was now down to just over 2 million, the short stack, tenth place. I didn't care who busted out first; I just hoped they'd do it soon so I could go back to my hotel and get some sleep.

Another two hours went by before Steven Garfinkle finally busted out. Within the first half hour, I knew I had the final table in hand. I drew a six-five off suit in the big blind. Normally I'd fold a hand like this or limp in with it from the big blind; I'd play it only if I didn't have to put any more money into the pot to see the flop.

The first eight players to act all folded.

That left Lee Childs and me. Again. Sometimes you get lucky with a hand like a six-five off suit in the big blind, a hand with a less than 5 percent chance of winning, and everyone folds to you, giving you the blinds and antes.

I didn't get lucky.

Lee Childs raised 600,000 from the small blind. I would have to put in one-tenth of my chips to keep playing a hand with a small chance of winning. Good poker strategy says to fold, but something inside of me told me to keep playing. I called.

The flop came, ten-eight-six, all of different suits. At least I now had a pair, albeit, the smallest pair possible based on the cards on the table. If Lee had made a big bet right then or possibly gone all in, I would have folded. An aggressive raise signals a large pocket pair. He didn't make a bet. Instead, he tapped on his chips, signaling a check.

I should have pushed hard and forced him to fold. But no one ever pushes hard with a pair of sixes when two potentially larger pairs are staring you in the face. I checked.

We both got to see the turn card for free, without risking any more of our chips. The dealer burned a card, then dealt the turn card: a four.

Lee bet 800,000. While that sounds like a lot, it really wasn't, not when you consider that it was less than half the pot size.

I stared at the cards on the table. *If Lee has a ten or an eight, I'm sunk,* I thought. *All I have is a lowly pair of sixes.* If my tournament life had been on the line, I would have folded. But I wasn't playing the cards; I was playing Lee Childs, and something about him told me he had nothing. "I call."

The pot was now slightly over 3 million.

The river came: an ace.

Lee was the first to act. "A million and a half."

It was what I'd been waiting for. If he'd had an ace, he would have bet at least 3 million, which would have doubled the pot and crippled me. Instead, his bet was more of a probe bet, a kind of dare to see what kind of hand I really had. With nearly 18 million in chips in front of him when this hand had begun, he could afford to throw out a measly million and a half to find out if I was bluffing.

I looked at the table. If he paired any one of the cards, he would have me beat. I looked at him. Again, something told me he didn't have an ace or a ten or an eight. I knew he didn't have anything that could hurt me. "I call."

I turned my lowly six-five.

Lee tossed his cards toward the dealer in disgust.

As soon as he did, I knew I would make the final table. I'd played a hand I probably should have folded, but my instincts had told me to keep going.

Texas Hold 'Em is a marathon, but it's also a test of courage. From time to time, you have to play a hand you normally wouldn't, and you have to stand your ground when inside you want to fold.

I had just proved to myself I could do both. I knew I would not only survive this day but make the final table.

Two hours later, at 4:15 a.m. on Monday, sixteen hours after play had begun, Raymond Rahme knocked out Steven Garfinkle. The final table was now set. Even though I was in eighth place with a chip stack barely over one-third the size of the chip leader Phil Hilm's, I had a shot. And once the first card is dealt at the final table, anything can happen.

15

A Place Where People Went to Die

Once we finally made it across the Mekong and into Thailand, I knew we were safe, but that was all I knew. Where we would live or find food or water was still a mystery. To be honest, it didn't matter to me at the time. Staying in Laos would've meant certain death or worse.

Many people in the West have heard of the killing fields in Cambodia, where the Communist Khmer Rouge tortured and killed over a million people. Similar crimes were committed in Laos by the Pathet Lao, albeit on a much smaller scale, only because the population was lower. The truth is that these atrocities continue today.[7]

The soldiers who found us on the shore of the Mekong escorted us to a makeshift camp just beyond the river. There, American Red Cross workers handed out blankets and Thai volunteers gave each of us a small bowl of rice and a piece of dried fish. Few meals in my life have ever tasted so good. I

7. Amnesty International reported specific incidents of innocent Hmong being massacred by the Lao Communist government as recently as 2006, thirty years after my family fled Laos (http://www.amnesty.org/en/library/asset/ASA26/002/2006/en/73e1366a-d434-11dd-8743-d305bea2b2c7/asa260022006en.html). They have also documented other acts of oppression up to the date of the writing of this book (http://www.amnesty.org/en/library/asset/ASA39/002/2009/en/5655ee8b-e6ee-11dd-a371-adcd1d2c1b57/asa390022009en.html).

hadn't eaten anything in a long time.

The instant I finished the meal, I asked, "Father, do you mind if I go see my friends from home?"

My father could hardly keep his eyes open. The fatigue of the past month appeared to hit him all at once. "No, Xao, go ahead, but don't get too far away."

I took off running to a group of people who looked familiar. "Bee," I yelled to one of my buddies, "let's play."

I didn't have to ask him twice.

The two of us rounded up the rest of our gang. I scratched out hopscotch lines in the dirt, and we played until we grew bored with it. Then we found a piece of rope and played tug-of-war. It felt so good to act like a child again.

On my way back to my family, I noticed all the adults in the camp wore the same weary, frightened looks. We may have been safe, but no one old enough to understand the situation could relax. Every person in the camp had left the only homes we'd ever known, the only lives we'd ever imagined.

Now we were strangers in an unfamiliar country. All around us, the landscape looked basically the same as it had on the Lao side of the Mekong, yet we didn't have houses or farms or any way of making a life for ourselves. Adding to the sense of unease was the fact that most of us, unlike my father, didn't speak Thai.

The river of people pouring into the temporary camp, both Hmong and Lao, slowed when the sun rose. It started up again the moment dusk fell. Whenever a new group arrived, questions started flying both directions.

"Have you seen my son?"

"Does anyone know where my father is?"

"I can't find my aunt. Can you help me?"

Stories always followed questions.

A weeping woman cried out, "They shot my husband right in front of me as we crossed the river."

Another told of watching friends drown in the Mekong.

Still another spoke of all the people from their village who'd died while trying to make it to the river.

The names and faces changed, but the stories were all very much the same.

New arrivals also brought news from home. Back when my village decided to flee for Thailand, one older man and his grown son had criticized my father's plan. Their families had stayed behind to take their chances with the Pathet Lao.

An acquaintance from a nearby village gave us an update. As soon as we had left, the criticizing man and his son had raided the cave vault under the waterfall. They had claimed all of our treasures, cattle, pigs, and fields. Within a matter of days, however, the Communist soldiers had executed every single member of their family.

Though these men had opposed my father so strongly, the news of their death made me very sad.

I knew if we'd stayed in Laos, none of us would have lived.

Within a day or two, the Thai government bussed us from the temporary camp to a large refugee camp at Nam Phong. Nam Phong had once been a secret Thai–United States commando training center for Hmong and Lao guerrilla fighters.

At the end of the Vietnam War, a United States Marine Aircraft Wing fighter squadron had flown missions from there.[8] The barracks were converted to refugee housing when the first wave of Hmong and Lao fled across the Mekong. By the time we arrived, those buildings had long since been filled.

Our bus pulled into Nam Phong about midnight. Tall poles with floodlights sprang up from every corner of the camp, illuminating the entire area.

"What is this?" I asked as we pulled up to the gate. I couldn't believe my eyes. Green tents stretched across the entire former military base. Between them, little children ran and played and adults milled about. "Doesn't anyone sleep here?"

"Don't worry about that, Xao," my father said. "Stick close to your mother and me."

The bus stopped, a door opened, and a Thai soldier entered, speaking words I couldn't understand.

My father had to translate for us. If I remember correctly, the soldier told us to follow him and not to touch any of the light poles because they weren't completely grounded and several people had been electrocuted when they'd accidentally run into them. "And be watchful for wild dogs," my father translated. "They roam the outskirts of the camp during the day and try to get inside at night. They carry disease and are very dangerous."

With its killer light poles and packs of wild dogs, this didn't sound like a safe place. I was scared.

My family stood in a long line to pick up more blankets and a few pieces of clothing from volunteers. An official-looking

---

8. Jane Hamilton-Merritt, *Tragic Mountains, the Hmong, the Americans, and the Secret Wars for Laos, 1942-1992*, p. 348.

man also handed my father an oversized bundle of dark green cloth, a long pole, and some stakes and rope. I hadn't seen anything like these items before, but my father knew what to do with them.

From the supply line, we made our way to the space assigned us within the Hmong section of the camp. My father and several other men worked for over an hour putting up a 30-by-20-foot tent in which five families, including ours, would spend the night.

Little did I know this tent would be our home for the next six months.

As soon as the sun came up, I took off to explore the camp with a couple of my buddies. We didn't stray far from our families, but we walked enough to get a good feel for life in our new community, which dwarfed our village in Laos. People, tens of thousands, filled every square foot of space. Like clockwork, every few hours more buses and trucks pulled in and new tents sprang up.

A walking path went straight between the endless rows of tents. Everywhere we went, we saw people walking, conversing. Some laughed; others cried. We heard people talking about lost relatives and those who had died trying to escape Laos. We couldn't escape the reality of what we'd just been through.

Around one corner, my buddies and I came upon some boys playing marbles with *real marbles*—not the rounded rocks we used but honest-to-goodness glass ball marbles.

"Take a look at that." I nudged one of my buddies.

"Wow. What I wouldn't give for one of those."

"Yeah, me too."

We could have bought some. Vendors prowled around the camp and sold anything anyone could want, including genuine glass marbles. However, since they didn't hand out free samples and neither my buddies nor I had any money, that didn't do my buddies and me much good.

For a while we watched the kids play marbles; then we went off exploring again. In another part of the camp, we saw boys playing with rubber bands, crouching on the ground, and drawing a line in the dirt. The first player flicked the inside top of his rubber band with his fingers and sent it past the line. The next player then flicked his toward the first player's. If the second band landed on top of the first, he took both. If he missed, the first player tried to land his on the other's. A couple of guys had a lot of rubber bands on their wrists, which looked so cool to me. I wanted to get some of my own.

My buddies and I covered quite a bit of the camp during our first few days in Nam Phong. We saw almost everything in the world there but never a school. The children in the camp had nothing to do except play games in the dirt.

The adults, too, had nothing to do except to cook the food the relief workers gave us. Each family was given a pot and some firewood or charcoal. Everyone cooked on top of a three-legged metal stand over a campfire.

While the women cooked, the men stood and talked or played checkers using Pepsi bottle caps. For men who'd always farmed and hunted and provided for their families, doing nothing was a difficult way of life.

For all of us, every day was exactly like the day before. We could only count the passing of the days waiting for no one knew what.

My father didn't want to see his children standing around doing nothing, so he made me and my older brother responsible for taking a large jar to the stream and filling it with water.

The stream was our only water supply. Everyone also did their wash and took baths there. That meant we had to boil the water before drinking it; otherwise, it made us sick.

In the camp, there was a lot of sickness—and death.

To this day, I am grateful to the Thai government for taking us in, but the magnitude of the number of refugees was more than any government could manage. Tens of thousands had fled Laos while masses of people had escaped Cambodia and even Vietnam.

With so many refugee camps and multitudes of people crammed into such small spaces, sickness and death were inevitable. Every sort of disease spread quickly through Nam Phong. We had to sleep under mosquito nets to try to protect ourselves from malaria. People got it anyway. Others came down with measles or polio or any other disease you can imagine.

It was not only disease that ended lives. People died when the wild dogs raided their tents, while those who survived the attacks died of rabies. Others died when they accidentally touched the light poles. People died every day: old men, babies, strangers, my cousins.

With death came the cry that still chills me. Every single day in the camp, from the first till the last, the air was filled with the loud, sorrowful cry as families carried bodies through the camp on their way to the cemetery. Every day was funeral day.

Death didn't always come because of sickness or accidents, either. One day relief workers passed out a bread called, in Thai, *qhob noom qhaij*, which is similar to a muffin or cinnamon roll. I got excited. Treats like this were rare.

However, before the bread made it as far as our little corner of Nam Phong, a warning soon spread. Part of the shipment of *qhob noom qhaij* had been poisoned. By the time the alert had gone out, a lot of people had already died.

No one ever discovered who'd poisoned the bread. I wished they had. From that day on, I remained wary of the food. It didn't stop me from eating it, though.

With so many refugees and more arriving every day, the camp always had a short supply of food. Some weeks we had plenty, relatively speaking; others we had next to none. The trucks were supposed to arrive every three days, but sometimes they didn't show up for four or five. By then their cargo was often rotten, but we had to eat it or starve.

One day, a truck filled with bananas came through Nam Phong. It didn't stop but drove along one of the camp roads while someone threw the fruit out the back to people chasing behind.

I loved bananas. I had to have one. I took off after the truck, but I could never get close enough to catch one. Stronger men ran faster than I could. When I'd almost gotten near enough to grab the prize, a man pushed me out of the way and sent me sprawling. The hard ground scraped the skin off my knee, a wound so deep that I still have the scar today. By the time I picked myself up, the truck was out of sight.

Dejected, I turned around and started back toward my tent. All of a sudden, I spotted a discarded banana on the ground. One end had been stepped on, but I didn't care. I broke the smashed part off and took the rest back to our tent, where I mixed it with my bowl of rice. It tasted so good.

The bathrooms of Nam Phong consisted of a hole in the ground covered by a board with an opening cut out of it. When you did your business, you stood or squatted and took aim.

One afternoon I went to the bathroom. My stomach hurt. Something didn't feel normal. I wiped and felt something hanging out of me. I tried to grab it but couldn't. Scared, I called for my brother. "Xay, help me. Something's wrong."

I knew what that something was.

My brother came running. When he saw me crouching there, tears running down my face, a worm dangling out of me, he said, "What can I do?"

Crying hard, I said, "Go grab a stick and break it in half, like chopsticks, and use it to pull the worm out."

My brother left for a moment and came back with a stick.

My idea worked. However, this would not be the last time I'd pass worms.

Such was life in the refugee camp.

After six months, buses moved my family from Nam Phong to Ban Vinai. Although it was certainly an upgrade, the same hopelessness and desperation hovered. Every day was like the day before: disease, desperation, boredom, death. Always death.

To my young mind this was where people went to die, and I wondered when it would be my turn.

16
The Happiest Day

I remember it as if it's happening at this very moment. When I close my eyes, I see everything again.

There is the wood and thatched roof apartment on the dirty hills of Ban Vinai where I've lived four years with my family. Below and to one side is the pond where my buddies and I swim, beyond that a field where we play. The refugee camp administration buildings stand on the edge of the field.

The sun is hot, the air humid, just as they are every day in Ban Vinai. I'm wearing my only pants: cut off a couple of times because of the holes I've worn into them, striped. I'm also wearing a Donald Duck shirt, though I have no idea who that is.

It's my turn to fill our jars with water from the community well. I've lowered the five-gallon bucket when the camp public address system crackles.

Then comes the voice. The voice of God? The only voice

that can give us hope of escape. "Attention: we have an announcement regarding the next group of people who will have interviews with the American consulate for an opportunity to go to America."

I stop to listen.

"Would the following people please report for interviews? Mr. Youa Lo Yang, district one, region one, apartment seven, room ten . . ."

The moment I hear my father's name, I jump up and take off running toward my house, forgetting all about the bucket. I guess it's at the bottom of the well, but I don't care.

Since coming to Ban Vinai, I've lived with only one hope: to hear my father's name over the camp intercom.

I'd never seen America, and I didn't know anyone who had besides the tall, strong-looking aid workers who handed out food and Donald Duck or Mickey Mouse T-shirts.

But I'd heard the stories of what America must be like. One of my uncles had once lived in the Lao capital, Vientiane. He used to tell the boys in the camp about life in the big city: the fancy buildings, the cars and trucks rushing up the roads, and the food. Oh, the city had lots and lots of food. "America has to be like Vientiane, but with much, much more of everything," he told us.

Before we arrived in Ban Vinai, I'd never even heard the word "America," but for the past four years it was all I could think about. *In America no one ever goes hungry or poops worms or wears beat-up old T-shirts with unknown cartoon characters on them. They all have new clothes and a chance to go to the finest schools in the world.* That's where I wanted to be: America, paradise.

When my family had first arrived in Ban Vinai in late 1975, tents had covered the entire complex, just as they had in Nam Phong. After a few weeks, trucks loaded with building materials had rumbled into the camp.

My father was especially glad to see those trucks because they meant work for him and a new home for his family. He and the other men immediately started building permanent housing for all of us.

Unlike the grand house we'd left in the mountains of Laos, this home was a small apartment. Apartment seven, room ten, to be exact.

The buildings sat on stilts on the side of a hill. To get to our apartment, we had to climb a tall stairway and walk on a balcony with no handrail. At first, I was afraid. I've never liked heights, and here there was nothing to keep me from falling.

Though I hated the height, this apartment was the nicest place I'd ever seen. It may have been smaller than our Laos home, but it was made of wood. Never before had I lived in a house made of wood. The apartment had only one room, which was about 20 by 15 feet, perhaps a little smaller.

My brother and I slept on mats in one corner, while my parents slept on the opposite side with my other brothers' and sister's mats between us. A curtain separated my parents' area from the rest of the house.

We'd lived in Ban Vinai about three months when we moved into the apartment. At the time, we didn't have anything except some blankets, a handful of pots, and a set of clothes for each family member.

The second I heard my family's name over the camp intercom, I ran as fast as I could up the dirt path to this apartment.

A couple of my buddies waved. They'd heard my name as well and knew exactly what it meant. For me, this was the happiest day. For my buddies, it was not. I knew because I'd been in their place.

About six months after we'd arrived in Ban Vinai, word had spread that France and the United States had opened their doors to Hmong refugees. People said all you had to do was submit your name and they would let you in.

It wasn't quite that simple for us. To get into the United States, you had to pass an intense interview process.

One of my uncles, who'd once lived in Vientiane, had tried to talk my father into moving to France. "That's where I'm going no matter what," he'd said. "The interview process is much easier, and French is simpler to learn than English."

My father wasn't persuaded. "I don't know anything about France, but I do know this: for thirteen years, I fought for America. They trained me and put a gun in my hand. I shed a lot of blood fighting against the North Vietnamese, and I watched many of my friends die. We all made huge sacrifices for America. No, you can go to France if you like, but I'm going to the United States of America. There is no discussion about that."

Representatives from both France and the United States had set up shop in the camp. True to his word, my father had filled out all the required paperwork for political asylum in America, not France.

He'd had to prove we'd fled Laos because our lives were in danger due to his serving in General Vang Pao's army. "America will honor the word they gave me," he'd said time and again.

When he'd first filled out the paperwork, I was excited. *We won't be here much longer.* More than three years had now passed, which meant we'd lived in refugee camps well over four. In that time, I'd heard the voice of God call over the intercom many, many names.

My uncle's name was called, and he and his family moved to France. Friends' names were called. Those days were very hard. I had to say good-bye to some of my buddies I'd known since we'd climbed trees in our village.

The most challenging day came when the intercom crackled and the voice called my father's younger brother's name. Not only did my uncle's family get to leave the camp and fly to America, but my grandmother would go with them.

The day the buses came for them, I could hardly control myself. After my birth mother had died, my grandmother had cared for me. I loved and admired her so. Now I had to say good-bye. I couldn't do it.

Our entire Yang clan escorted my uncle and his family and my grandmother to the buses. Right before she boarded, my grandmother hugged me and said good-bye. My father had to pry my arms from her neck. Even after she took her seat on the bus, I reached up as high as I could toward her window.

She took hold of my hand. "It will be okay, Xao. You will

join me in America very soon."

I couldn't say anything. Tears flowed down my face.

When the bus started moving toward the camp gate, I was still holding on to my grandmother's hand. I ran alongside but lost my grip. I fell in the dust and cried until my father picked me up and led me back to apartment seven, room ten.

Six months had passed since that day. Now as I sprinted across Ban Vinai toward home, it hit me, *I will get to see my grandmother again soon.* The thought made me so happy that I think my feet actually lifted off the ground and I began flying toward the apartment.

My grandmother and my uncle's family had settled in a place called Nashville in something called Tennessee. I assumed we would go there as well. In order for a Hmong refugee family to be allowed into the United States, someone there had to commit to be their sponsor. No doubt my uncle had found a sponsor for us in this place called Nashville. Whatever Nashville and Tennessee might be, I knew they had to be better than Ban Vinai.

When I reached our building, I raced up the stairs and darted down the balcony, not even thinking about the height. I burst into our room and nearly shouted, "Did you hear that? They called our name. We have an interview. We're going to America."

"No," my mother said, "we didn't hear anything. Are you sure you heard it correctly?"

"Sure, I'm sure," I shouted.

"I will go and check this out," my father said. "Stay here with your mother, Xao. I will be right back." My father darted out the door toward the camp administration buildings. I could tell from the way he walked that he was as excited as I was. Who wouldn't be?

"Did you bring the water, Xao?" my mother asked.

Water? Who cares about water at a time like this? "No, ma'am. I guess in all the excitement, I forgot it."

"Stay here with your brothers. I'll go next door and get some," she said.

I sat next to my little brother. "We're finally going to get to leave here."

But not all of us, I thought. I looked around our small apartment. So much had happened here in the past four years.

My mind wandered to a day in 1977, two years after we'd arrived in the camp, when my little sister woke up complaining of a stomachache. With so little food and so much sickness, her symptoms were not uncommon.

My sister's stomachache grew so bad that my father took her to the health clinic the Thai government had built. For the camp's population of approximately 50,000 refugees, the clinic had only one or two doctors and a handful of trained nurses.

My sister was given some medicine, but it didn't help. Then one day she woke up with a purplish color to her skin. She was in so much pain. All she could do was cry. Throughout the night and all during the day for nearly a week, she cried. My parents tried so hard to help her, but they didn't know what to do.

Then she left us.

My parents dressed her in her finest clothes and carried

her through the camp while we sang hymns.

We buried her body in the cemetery on the edge of Ban Vinai.

Then I thought about my baby brother, who'd died two years later. He'd been born in the camp, right here in our apartment, a short time before my sister had become ill. My father delivered the baby himself, just as he had delivered me and my brothers and sister.

Oh, my baby brother was so small, so young when he passed.

Merely five or six months had gone by since we'd lost my brother. I couldn't help but think that if he and my sister had survived a little while longer, until we were allowed to go to America, they might have been all right. I couldn't imagine children dying in America.

I wanted to be able to do something someday to help people like us. I planned to become a doctor. I knew that meant a lot of schooling, but I believed if I could ever get the chance, I could do it.

We had a school in Ban Vinai, and all the children went there every day from eight in the morning until two in the afternoon. I learned to read and write in both Lao and Thai. I did so well that my teacher let me skip the second grade. That made my father proud.

However, I don't mean to mislead you into thinking I became a serious student while living in Ban Vinai. The Tom Sawyer in me kept coming out. I had to find a way to have fun.

From time to time, the Thai officials running the camp set up an outdoor movie theater in the large field where we played soccer. Unfortunately, it cost money to get into the movies, and neither I nor any of my friends had any. The theater consisted of tall sheets stretched out between poles, one of which served as the movie screen.

Walls of cloth couldn't stop my buddies and me. We waited until no one was looking and crawled under the sheet walls and then mixed in with the crowd. After all, who'd notice four or five little boys?

And who could blame us for wanting to sneak inside? They showed Jackie Chan movies there. Every little boy loves Jackie Chan. I will never forget the first movie I ever saw: *Snake in the Eagle's Shadow.* Jackie was great in that one. Today I own the DVD; it brings back such great memories.

Before long, we were caught and security guards were stationed around the theater to keep us out. To me, it made seeing the movie that much more of a challenge—and I love challenges.

One particular movie night, the three of us remaining in Ban Vinai from our original gang noticed a woman wearing a long, flowing dress. It looked like something out of the movies.

I motioned for my buddies. "Follow me, and do what I do." I slipped through the crowd until I was right behind the woman in the dress. With so many people milling about waiting for the movie to begin, no one paid any attention to me or my friends. I crouched behind the woman, then ducked underneath her dress, the other two trying to follow me. My plan was for the three of us to duckwalk under the dress all the way into the theater.

We might have made it, except one of us tripped, which

sent the other two sprawling. Then I rolled onto the woman's dress, which nearly pulled her on top of us.

The next thing I knew, a security guard was glaring at the three of us, while the woman yelled.

My buddies and I laughed so hard we nearly hurt ourselves.

After that, we contented ourselves with watching the movie from a distance while perched high in the nearby trees. It was the perfect view. I couldn't hear the movie, but who needs sound when you have kung fu fighting?

During the day, we swam in the camp's large lake, played marbles, or flipped rubber bands. We also invented a game where we flipped Pepsi caps. None of us had any real toys aside from some little something or other that we won as a prize at school. That didn't stop us from finding ways to have fun. Even in this place filled with so much death and helplessness, children always found a way to play. I guess that's what enabled us to survive.

My father came running back into our apartment, almost shouting, "Xao was right. We definitely have an interview."

"And then we go to America?" I said.

"First we must pass the interview," he said, trying to calm me.

"And then America?"

"If we pass the interview, yes, then America."

I jumped and shouted. I'd never heard such good news.

17

Free at Last

Our interview with the Americans came one long month after the happiest day of my life. The entire family had to be interviewed together. My father had drilled us so we'd know how to respond and when to stay silent.

You must understand, all 50,000 refugees in Ban Vinai would do and say anything to get to America, but not just anyone could get in. It was not enough that you were Hmong and your life was endangered by the Pathet Lao; you had to prove you were genuinely a political refugee because you'd joined the fight against the Communists on behalf of the United States.

The American representative must have heard all sorts of wild stories from people desperate to get out of Ban Vinai.

Because record keeping in General Vang Pao's army had left much to be desired, my father had to answer some very specific questions about the weapons he'd used in order to prove he'd actually fought for America. I stood next to him as he explained the firing capabilities of the M-1s and M-16s.

The American representative also asked him to describe the mission when my father had rescued the downed American pilot. "And what was the pilot's name?" he asked through an interpreter.

"I don't know."

My heart sank. I was afraid he might not believe any of the story.

My father didn't panic in the least. "When I led my men through the jungle to the downed pilot, all I cared about was getting to him before the Communists did and taking him out of harm's way. The pilot didn't speak Hmong, and I don't speak English. Even if he had told me his name, I wouldn't have been able to understand it. Besides, I didn't have a chance to sit with him for a long chat. The second we got him back to our base, a helicopter swept down and carried him away."

The American made a few notes and gave a slight smile.

I relaxed a little, until the interpreter asked the next question.

"All of your children look like you, except these two." He pointed at my younger brother, Kham Dy, and me. "They have very round faces, different from yours and your wife's."

What? How could this man question whether he's my father? Of course he's my father. For a moment, I feared they might try to separate me from my parents and leave my brother and me in Ban Vinai.

"I'm only a human being," my father replied. "God gave me these children, and I accept them just the way they are. They may not look like me, but I have no control over that. Only God does."

I loved his answer.

The interviewer, however, pressed further. Turning to my brother, he said, "Is this really your mother and father?"

"Yes."

Before the interview, my father had told all of us to give succinct answers.

Then the interviewer turned to me. "Is this your father and your mother?"

"Yes."

My father didn't explain to the man that our real mother had died during childbirth when I was three. I think he was afraid something might get lost in translation and the interviewer might get the wrong idea about us. The man conducting the interview had lived in Laos as part of the CIA and knew polygamy was common in our culture. My father didn't want to give someone the opportunity to jump to the conclusion that he had multiple wives.

As it turned out, he didn't need to worry. We passed the interview and were scheduled to leave for the United States with the next group.

Leaving Ban Vinai proved to be harder for my father than I ever would have imagined.

Me? I couldn't wait to get out of there, though I hated the thought of leaving behind the last two members of my old gang.

For my father, leaving meant doing something he never had before. All my life I'd watched as he put the needs of the people of his village above his and his family's. When we'd escaped through the jungle, our family had taken up the rear. When we'd jumped into the trucks in Num Chang, my father had made sure everyone was on board before he and two of his young sons were. When we'd crossed the Mekong, everyone else was safely on the Thai shore before our family ever climbed into a boat.

This time, however, my father had no choice but to leave some of his people behind. The night before we left Ban Vinai, he gathered the few who remained from our village. Many of our people had already gone to America, while some had not survived the years in the camps.

The scene reminded me of the night the entire village had gathered in our house in Laos when we'd made the decision to escape through the jungle. Back then, I'd felt as if my father was Moses getting ready to lead his people out of their slavery in Egypt. Now, four and a half years later, my family stood on the brink of entering the promised land while others had to stay behind in the wilderness.

The last two members of my gang, my buddies Bee and Yer, came to the meeting on my family's last night in Ban Vinai. I couldn't bring myself to think we might never see one another again.

Bee asked, "Xao, when you get to America, do you think you can send me some money?"

"Of course." I firmly believed I'd have so much of everything in America that I could easily spare a few dollars to send to my best friends.

Then, looking out on those who remained from our village,

my father spoke. "Since long ago in Laos, I have always tried to do what was best for you. I have led you the best I knew how. Tomorrow, we will part. I pray we will see each other again on this side of heaven. Until we do, be strong. Do not give up hope. God is here, and He will continue to take care of you."

Many tears and good-byes followed.

Bee, Yer, and I stayed up most of the night talking about the good times we'd had. We didn't mention the bad times. They didn't seem so important right then.

I gave my buddies my extensive rubber band collection. As it turned out, I'd become the best rubber band player in the camp, at least in our little corner of it.

I also gave them the plastic bag full of bones I'd buried. Every so often, a group of men had come through the camp and collected all the leftover animal bones from the food we'd been given. They'd given us candy in exchange for them. I wasn't sure why. Word around camp said the men sold the bones to a company that ground them into a powder used in a meat tenderizer. Neither my buddies nor I cared what the men did with them. All we knew was that we could trade them for candy, and we loved candy. Now my friends could enjoy some, my treat.

Finally, morning came. I woke up so excited I could hardly hold still. I ran to the shelf where my parents stored all the important items, but it was pretty bare. My parents had given away everything we weren't taking to America.

High on the shelf was a box, and in the box was something that belonged to me. After our interview, my uncle in America had sent my father $50. With that money, my father had purchased a large amount of fabric for new clothes for all of us. A tailor in the camp had made me the most spectacular pair of pants I could have imagined. They even had bell-bottoms.

In the camp, I'd worn whatever old clothes the relief agencies had handed out, most of them ragged even before I'd gotten them. Not these pants! They were new, a first for me. In the weeks leading to our departure, I'd pulled them off the shelf and stared at them in wonder.

Today was different. I pulled them off the shelf and put them on. I also put on something I'd never worn before: shoes. A cousin had given me this pair after he'd left for America. One side had been torn out, but my father had given me a little money so I could have them repaired. I also put on my best shirt, the only one I planned to take with me to America.

I can't describe the feeling that came over me as I stood there, dressed in the finest pants money could buy, my best shirt, and actual shoes, ready to head to America. *This must be how the Israelites felt the day they entered the land of milk and honey*, I thought. *Soon I'll have a different set of clothes for every day of the week and all the food I could ever want. I won't be poor or hungry. I will never have to struggle again.*

A large crowd arrived at our apartment to escort us to the buses. All across the camp, similar scenes played out. Six months earlier, our family had been part of the crowd escorting my uncle and grandmother to the buses. Now it was our turn to leave.

My buddies Bee and Yer pushed through the crowd to get

to me. "You won't forget us, will you?" one asked.

"How could I ever forget the two of you?"

We walked arm in arm up the hill. At the crest, I looked down to see twenty or twenty-five buses lined up like a long caterpillar on the far side of the camp. People filled the soccer field between me and the buses. Beyond that, I saw people hanging out of the buses, holding the hands of people beside, just like my grandmother had held on to mine until the bus had left.

This is real. This is finally happening to me. I'm going to America for sure this time.

I knew the buses would take us only as far as Bangkok. From there, we had to take an airplane to America. I had no idea how long the trip would take, and I didn't care.

Once we got to the buses, my father said to my family, "Wait here while I find out which bus is ours."

Bee and Yer grabbed me even tighter. Tears ran down our faces. None of us could bring ourselves to say anything.

"We're on bus eight," my father said after a few moments.

I liked the sound of that. In Asia, eight is the luckiest number.

Bee, Yer, and I walked to the bus. Even after I arrived at the door, we didn't want to let go.

I couldn't bring myself to say good-bye.

Finally, my father said, "Boys, it's time. We need to get on the bus. Xao, say your good-byes, and let's go. We have no choice."

I looked at my two buddies. I could imagine the three of us along with the rest of our gang, running around the chicken coop, smashing eggs, or racing to the waterfall near our village on a hot summer day. I couldn't wrap my mind around the fact that this was it. I was leaving my best friends.

"Xao," my father said. "It's time. We need to get on the bus."

I pulled myself away. "I will see you later." I hoped against hope it was true.

It felt like a funeral. Because of the hope I had in Jesus, I knew we'd meet in heaven someday, but I hoped we'd see each other before then.

After I got on the bus, my father said, "You and Xay sit here on the front row."

We jumped into our seat, while my mother and two younger brothers took the one behind us. My father and brother Kham Dy sat behind them in the third row.

From outside the bus came the sound of wailing as loved ones said their good-byes.

I looked at the open door. Every so often, Bee and Yer peeked in for one last look at me. I turned around and looked at my mother and father. Both of them were leaning out the window, talking with my widowed aunts.

Everyone cried. All of us on the bus were so sad to leave our loved ones behind, yet we couldn't wait to get out of Ban Vinai.

After what seemed like forever, the door closed and the bus started rolling forward. Just as on the day my grandmother had left, people ran alongside the bus, holding on to their loved ones' hands as long as they could.

From a loudspeaker outside, we heard, "Please stand clear of the buses. We don't want anyone to get hurt."

No one listened. I watched as my aunts held on till their legs couldn't keep up with the buses. Just like that, they disappeared.

As the buses wound their way up a hill toward the camp entrance, I looked out. High in the distance sat apartment number ten, room seven, as if it were waiting for us to come back.

My mind flashed back to the day I'd looked at my village in Laos one last time before we'd headed into the jungle, never to return. For four years, I'd thought Ban Vinai was a place where people went to die. I'd prayed our family would escape, but a part of me had doubted it would ever happen.

Now the bus picked up speed. I settled into my seat and smiled even as the last few tears streamed down.

Up ahead I saw a small security station at the camp entrance. I'd never been this close to it before. A long bar stretched across the road, blocking the gate. As soon as the first bus came to the bar, it swung up and let them pass.

My heart beat faster as we drove closer and closer. Finally, we passed underneath the bar and out the gate.

A sense of relief washed over me. I felt like a new person.

When we'd first stepped on the Thai shore of the Mekong, I'd thought I was free. Now, four and a half years later, I was. At last.

18

On the Cusp of a Dream

"This is the last time. I promise." The World Series of Poker official laughed as he handed me the plastic bag for my chips along with the triplicate form where I'd record my total.

"Thank you." I stared at the bag a moment, a wave of fatigue hitting me. For the first time, I felt every one of the sixteen hours of continuous poker I'd just played. I sat to count my chips.

Throughout the tournament, the dealers trade out the smaller denominations for ever larger ones. This meant that even though my stack had a much higher total value than the one I'd had after the first day, my total number of plastic chips was not that different.

"Wow. Unbelievable." I wrote the total on the form with two carbon copies, dropped one slip in with the chips, sealed the bag, and handed it to the tournament official. Then I handed one slip to the dealer and kept one for myself.

"Thanks, Jerry, and congratulations. You've played a great

tournament. Best of luck to you tomorrow."

"Thank you, my friend." I sighed. "Final table. Who would have ever believed this, right?"

He laughed. "Don't sell yourself short. No one gets this far by luck alone. Now go get some rest. You look like you need it."

"Yes, I am very tired." It was a huge understatement. I'd played sixteen hours of poker after a night of little sleep. I felt as if I could lie down right there on the poker table and fall asleep. At the same time, I had so much adrenaline pumping that I felt as if I could start play at the final table right then.

I looked at my chip count once again: 8.45 million. *And I couldn't believe it when I had 99,700 the first day. This is incredible.* Before I got too carried away with patting myself on the back, another thought occurred to me: *Of course, you are 14 million behind Philip Hilm.*

Having taken care of my poker business, I wanted to get to my car as quickly as possible to drive to my hotel.

I hadn't even left the area surrounding the feature table when a stranger stopped me. "Mr. Yang, Jerry, congratulations on making the final table. You played a whale of a tourney so far. You may not realize it yet, but your life is going to change from this point forward. That's where I can help. I'm an agent, and I would love to represent you—"

"Thank you"—I cut him off—"but I don't have time to speak with you now. If you'll give me your card, I'll be happy to get back with you later."

He tried to keep talking, but I politely excused myself and

kept walking.

No sooner had I brushed off the first agent than another stepped up and went into the same speech.

Then another.

And another.

I don't fault them. They were just doing their jobs, but it was too late, or too early, depending on how you look at the clock, for that kind of business.

Agents weren't the only ones trailing me out of the Amazon Room. All of the final table players were scheduled to appear at a press conference Monday at noon, which was now about seven hours away. In the meantime, a few reporters wanted a comment from me as they finished their stories on day six.

"Jerry," one of them asked, a tape recorder in his hand and a cameraman trailing behind, "how do you feel as you reach the top of an improbable climb?"

I slowed a little but didn't stop. "I am very pleased and excited." To be honest, my mind was so fatigued that I was surprised I could squeeze out a coherent sentence.

A couple other reporters asked variations of the same question, and I gave them basically the same answers.

I could see the door ahead, and I just wanted to get through it. Unlike all the other eight remaining players, I couldn't just duck into the nearest elevator. I had to go all the way across the casino to the parking garage, then drive another twenty minutes to my hotel.

Finally, the last reporter asked his question, and the last agent thrust his card into my hand. They could have kept following, but all of them were polite enough to stop once I reached the door.

At long last, I made it to my car, unlocked the door, and sat in the silence.

That's when it hit me. *Jerry Yang, in a little more than twenty-four hours, you are going to sit at the final table of the biggest, most important poker tournament in the world. You made it.*

I let out a little cheer, then pulled out my cell phone. I'd wanted to make this call since Steven Garfinkle had busted out a little more than half an hour earlier.

Even though it was the middle of the night, she picked up the phone on the first ring.

"Daddy?"

"Mommy, I did it. I made the final table."

Sue let out a scream. "I can't believe it. I mean, I can believe it, but I can't believe it!"

"Neither can I. I want you and the kids to come to Las Vegas to share this moment with me."

"Can we afford that, Daddy?"

I laughed. "Yes, Mommy, we can afford it." Ninth place was guaranteed over half a million dollars. "I booked a suite for everyone at the Rio, the same hotel where I'm playing. My parents are already staying in one of the bedrooms. You and I will stay in the other, and the kids will sleep in the living room. Make sure you bring their sleeping bags."

"I can't wait to come, but I hate the thought of driving that far by myself."

"You don't have to. I spoke with Pat Wilmes from the

Lake Elsinore Hotel & Casino earlier today. He wants you and the kids to be here with me. His casino has arranged for a limo to pick you up at the house and drive you all the way to Las Vegas."

"Nooo. Really?"

"And guess what? That's not all. They're also going to give you $2,500 spending money."

"What? Oh my, Daddy. That's about the nicest thing any-one has ever done for me."

"I know, I know. Oh, Mommy, I cannot wait for you to get here. I have missed you and the children so much."

I fought back tears and could tell Sue did as well. There was plenty of time for that later.

We talked for a little while as I drove back downtown. When I reached my hotel, I told her I loved her and would see her in a few hours. I couldn't wait.

The sun was coming up by the time I finally made it to my room to sleep. I walked in, tossed my jacket on the bed, then fell facedown on that smelly carpet and thanked my God for all He had done for me thus far. I knew He had a greater purpose in all of this than simply a poker tournament.

Then I tried to sleep, without much success. Though my body kept screaming to shut it down for now, my mind had other ideas. Every time I closed my eyes, I saw cards hitting the felt. I replayed dozens and dozens of hands.

Once I'd replayed all of day six, my thoughts turned to money. Wow, the money. Even if I were the first one to bust out, even if I went all in on the first hand and lost, I was guaranteed no less than $525,000.

Even after I pay out all the taxes, that still leaves more than enough to pay off the house and the car and put some into savings. But first I'll make good on the vow I made to the Lord a long time ago to use the money for good.

The thought made sleep that much more difficult. Now, not only did I have strategy to ponder and opponents to figure out, but my mind began racing with possible places to give one-tenth of whatever I won. The more my mind and body fought, the more thankful I was that I had to get up soon.

I had hardly slept at all by the time my alarm sounded. Though I had the day off, this would prove to be one of the busiest days of the tournament for me.

Before any of that, I would have to check out of my hotel. With my family coming to Las Vegas, it was time to move to a decent hotel. I looked around my smelly, dingy, poorly lit room as I packed my suitcase. *I'm actually going to miss this place.*

I could have changed hotels at any time after qualifying for the money on day three, but every time I went back to my room I felt a little like Rocky in *Rocky IV*, who trained in a run-down barn to keep his focus while his Russian opponent stayed in a fancy resort. *This is my old barn, so I guess that makes me Rocky.* I laughed.

After packing my bags, I took one last look around my room. "Thank you," I said to the empty space. "You kept me focused. I don't think I could have made it this far without you."

I arrived at the Amazon Room in time for the noon joint press conference with all of the final table contestants. Then each of us rotated through several different media rooms for one-on-one interviews with ESPN, *USA TODAY*, local Las Vegas television stations, and foreign press.

Even though I was an amateur, the press had lots of questions for me. Usually, the question came down to a variation of this: "Jerry, amateur players have won the past four World Series of Poker main events in a row. Can you be the fifth?"

I always gave the same answer: "I have a great deal of respect for the pros. Tomorrow I will do my best and hope the cards fall my way."

What else could I say?

After answering the last question, I went upstairs to the two-bedroom suite I'd rented for my parents. The moment I opened the door, my six children rushed at me.

"Daddy," they yelled, each one grabbing me.

I loved every second of it. I gave out hugs and kisses and more hugs and kisses. My two youngest children would barely let go.

Sue stood back, letting the children have their time.

"Kids, did Mommy tell you I made the final table?"

"You did?" my oldest daughter asked with that hint of sarcasm only a thirteen-year-old girl can muster.

I laughed so hard. "Of course. Why do you think you're here?"

I finally waded through the sea of our children and made it to my wife to wrap my arms around her. "Mommy, this is real. This is happening. In less than twenty-four hours, I'll play the final table." My emotions spilled out; I couldn't hold back the tears any longer.

"I know." Tears streamed down her face.

We stayed like that for a few minutes, holding one another, crying, while our children darted in and out around us.

Finally, Sue stood back. "And how much money does this mean you will win?"

I laughed so hard I could hardly answer.

Even though my family was now with me, I had to be alone for a while to plot my strategy for the next day. Of the eight other players remaining, I regarded three as the most dangerous: Philip Hilm, Lee Watkinson, and Alex Kravchenko.

Philip not only had the chip lead; he also was a fearless player.

I knew how good Lee Watkinson was because I'd watched him on television. Most of the poker experts regarded him as the best contender at the final table.

Even though Alex Kravchenko had the short stack, I knew firsthand how dangerous he could be. He'd been the short stack through most of day six, yet he'd survived. Of my eight opponents, he was perhaps the most disciplined, the most patient, and the hardest to eliminate.

As I prepared for the final table, I believed I had to take out these three to have any chance at winning. I mean no disrespect to the others; in fact, I think most of them would name the same three as their toughest opponents. Certainly, no one would have put Jerry Yang on that list.

In the previous two years, I'd watched and rewatched many professional players, including Lee Watkinson, on tele-

vision and made careful notes. On days five and six here, I'd
started taking notes on the players as well. The night before the
final table, I'd pulled out my notes one last time and studied.

Unless the other players had snuck into the Pechanga or
Lake Elsinore casinos and watched me in my local weekend
tournaments, they didn't have any notes on me beyond their
observations during the World Series of Poker.

I'd played at the same table as some of them, giving them
a read on me and vice versa. However, one's style of play and
approach to the game are different at the final table than they
are in the earlier rounds.

The fact that I'd watched Lee Watkinson play final tables
on television gave me just a little more information about him
than he had on me. And when it comes to Texas Hold 'Em, sometimes a little extra information can make all the difference.

I didn't sleep much better the night before the biggest day of
poker of my life. The children spread sleeping bags out across
the suite's living room. One or two may have crawled between
my parents in their bed.

Sue and I managed to keep everyone out of our room. It
was our first chance to really talk since I'd come to Las Vegas
twelve days earlier. For most of the night, we talked about how
our lives were about to change.

"Mommy, no matter what happens, you'll be able to be a
stay-at-home mom just like you've always wanted. Even if I'm
the first one out, we'll be able to pay off everything and live on
my salary alone."

I cannot tell you how long I'd dreamed of being able to make that happen.

I also talked poker strategy, which she didn't understand, but that didn't matter. It helped me just to have her listen.

Sue caught me up on everything that had taken place at home since I'd left for Vegas. With six children, there's always something happening in our house.

We discussed who we wanted to keep the children while I played poker the next day. I needed Sue in the Amazon Room with me. Most of our extended family either had already arrived or were on their way to Las Vegas. We had plenty of babysitters to choose from.

And we talked about giving one-tenth of whatever I won to a very good cause. Both of us knew we must use the money for something bigger than ourselves.

Sue and I talked and talked some more. We'd been apart too long. Both of us eventually drifted to sleep in the middle of our conversation.

Before I knew it, the alarm rang. Six o'clock had come so quickly.

Even before my feet hit the floor, the adrenaline was pumping. Perhaps I should have been more nervous. A queasy feeling hit me, but I also felt incredibly calm as I contemplated the day ahead.

No one ever anticipated I'd come so far. No matter what happened, I was already a winner. Yet I knew in my heart of hearts I didn't want to settle for ninth place any more than

I'd wanted to settle for the experience of having played in the World Series of Poker on day one.

"Mommy, I truly believe I can win this thing. I think I can do it."

"I know you can, Daddy. I *know* you can." She gave me a look, one different from the one she'd shot across the room two short years earlier. I could see in her eyes she truly believed what she said. I was ready, not merely to play but to win.

19
Landing in Paradise

The bus ride from Ban Vinai to Bangkok turned out to be less fairy tale and more like the life we Yangs had come to expect. About halfway there, the bus in front of us braked for a narrow bridge. I don't know if our driver wasn't paying attention or if he simply wasn't looking at that moment, but he didn't slow down and our bus slammed into the one ahead. No one was hurt, but the force of the collision knocked out our windshield.

Not long after that, a heavy rain began to fall. Since we were on the front row, my brother and I rode the rest of the way with the wind and rain blowing over us. By the time we finally arrived in Bangkok, both of us were on the verge of getting sick.

My father didn't want to take the chance of a cold delaying our trip the rest of the way to the United States, so once we settled into the dorm-like room in Bangkok, he pulled out a needle and said, "Xao, Xay, come over here and lie down."

I knew what he was going to do: a traditional Hmong healing technique that I hated, though it always seemed to work.

My father had each of us sit on the floor next to a warm bowl of water. He dipped his hands in, clapped them, then pushed on our stomachs and out toward our arms. Back and forth he went, from the stomach to the arm, pushing the bad blood away from the core of the body. He then tied a string around each wrist and applied pressure up each finger. Finally, once all the bad blood was concentrated in the tips of our fingers, with a needle he poked below each fingernail and squeezed the blood out. Once all the bad blood was out, he dipped our fingers into the warm water. Finally, he scraped off the top layer of each nail with a knife and sent us to bed. I don't know how one might explain it medically, but the procedure made me feel a lot better.

This was not the last time I was poked with a needle while in Bangkok. For the next three days, teams of doctors and nurses poked and prodded and peeked into every part of my body. Even though the medical staff at Ban Vinai had given us many immunizations through the years, apparently the United States required even more. My arm felt like a pincushion. They also ran tests on us to make sure we didn't have diseases like TB or worms.

The day of testing lasted forever. To make matters worse, they didn't allow us to eat until they were finished.

Oh, I was so hungry. *Just think, Xao, soon you'll land in America and have all the food you want.*

On our third day in Bangkok, a bus pulled up in front of

our dormitory.

"This is it," my father told us. "We're going to the airport to get on an airplane for America."

I'd never seen a plane up close. The nearest I'd ever come was watching the MiG fighters buzz over our village in Laos.

From the outside, the airport looked like all the other buildings we'd been herded in and out of the past few days. The Thai officials led us through the ticketing area and security as a group, then into a room to wait. For three days we'd played a variation of this game, moving from room to room, waiting to be told what to do.

After about an hour, our hosts herded us through a long hallway into another room with small, round windows and rows of three chairs on each side and of another five or six in the middle.

Our escort seated us in the middle section, which meant I couldn't see out the window. The chair, however, was quite comfortable, much more so than those in all the other waiting areas.

Voices came through the intercom, but I didn't know what they were talking about. A short time later, my chair began to rock just a little. The windows were too small for me to really view much, but it looked like we were moving.

A nice woman in a uniform said in Thai, "Please buckle your seat belts."

"What?"

She reached down, pulled the belts from both sides of my seat, and buckled them together.

I thanked her, then said, "Is this room moving?"

She smiled. "Why, yes, it is. The pilot just pulled away from the gate. We should be in the air soon."

"This is the airplane?"

"Yes, of course." She left to assist other passengers.

I wanted to run to the window to see what was really happening, but I couldn't because of the seat belt. The plane made a rumbling, and I found myself pressed against my seat. Finally, the shaking stopped and the noise around me changed.

"Are we flying?" I asked my father.

"Yes, Xao, we are flying." He laughed.

A short time later, a bell dinged.

"You can get up now," my father said to me and my brothers.

Most of the seats on either side of us were empty. My brothers and I jumped up and rushed to a nearby window.

"Wow," Xay said, "can you believe this? We're on top of the clouds."

I laughed. "I know. I never dreamed you could look down on the clouds. This is so cool."

We stared out that window forever. Well, until the flight attendants came with food. I didn't want to miss out on the food!

I know people used to complain about airplane food, back when airlines still served meals, but to me as a twelve-year-old boy who'd spent his entire life hungry, eating half-rotten food in a refugee camp for years, airplane food was gourmet dining at its best.

Still, something on my plate didn't look edible. It was red but clear, and it jiggled with the rocking of the plane.

When the flight attendant came by, I asked, "What is this?"

"Jell-O."

"Is it food? I don't think I should eat it."

She laughed. "Oh, yes, it's food. Try it. I think you'll like it."

I scooped up a little on my spoon. It looked even stranger close up. I sniffed it. *Hmmm, it smells kind of fruity.* Then I tasted it. *Oh my. Where has this been all my life? I love this Jell-O stuff.*

To wash everything down, I had a small brown carton with some liquid in it. I was reluctant to try it and had no idea how to open it.

On her next pass through the cabin, the flight attendant noticed my hesitation. "It's okay. Here, let me open it for you."

As with the Jell-O, I sniffed the drink first. Then I took a swig. "Wow, what do you call this stuff?"

"Chocolate milk."

"It feels like a party in my mouth." I nudged my brother. "Xay, this is it. We're going to eat like this from now on. If this is how they eat there, I think I'm going to enjoy America."

My brother's mouth was half full of Jell-O. "Meeeee toooooooooo."

Our flight from Bangkok to San Francisco lasted over seventeen hours. Thankfully, with so few passengers on board, my brothers and I were able to stretch out on the seats and sleep.

A few hours into the flight, I needed to go to the bathroom. My oldest brother had gone earlier, so I asked him, "Where's the bathroom?"

"Down this aisle toward the back. It's a little room. You will see it."

I found it all right, but when I walked in and closed the door, I wasn't sure what to do. The hole was up off the ground, and the board covering it didn't look stable. *This doesn't make a lot of sense,* I thought.

This was the first of many culture shocks awaiting me.

The plane felt as if it was slowing when the pilot's voice came through the intercom to announce in Thai that we would soon land in San Francisco. My brothers and I pressed our faces against the window and looked at the most glorious sight I'd ever seen. The Bible book of Revelation describes heaven as a city with streets of gold. Looking down on the Golden Gate Bridge and the Transamerica Pyramid, along with the brilliant green grass and the rolling hills leading to the bay below, I thought this had to be what the Bible had in mind.

"So beautiful," one of my brothers said.

"I can't wait to see it up close." I grinned.

After we'd landed, our escorts led us through the terminal to a waiting shuttle bus.

Wide-eyed, I looked at all the people in the airport. They were all so tall, the ladies so beautiful. I couldn't get over the first blonde woman I saw. I'd never imagined anyone could have that hair color.

The shuttle took us to a hotel where we stayed while our paperwork was processed. Our hosts led us into a banquet room, where a buffet awaited us.

Xay and I walked toward a large pot filled with noodles

covered in some sort of red stuff with lumps of meat sticking up.

"Xay, look at that. They covered the noodles in blood. That's disgusting."

"It doesn't smell like blood," he said. "Look, the Americans are already eating it. We should give it a try."

"I will if you will." With that, I took my first bite of spaghetti and meatballs. "Hmmmm, this isn't bad at all."

The staff also served us salad and fruit. I recognized the bananas and oranges but didn't know what to make of the orange-sized fruit with the smooth, red skin. I took a bite and liked it. Later, someone told me it was an apple.

The one fruit that really caught my eye was small and round and came in bunches. Some were red, some black, some green. I pulled off a red one and ate it. It tasted like candy— the best I'd ever had. I grabbed another and stared at it a moment. "What kind of fruit is this, and why is it so sweet? Do they soak these in sugar?"

"No," I was told through an interpreter, "they're naturally sweet. They're called grapes."

I ate grapes until I felt sick, and then I kept on eating them. Pure joy swept over me. *This is the America I dreamed about.* I also ate more Jell-O. Lots and lots of Jell-O. For dessert, I had my first ever chocolate chip cookie. I'm still a big fan.

After our meal, my father went to take care of our paperwork while our escort took Xay, Kham Dy, and me to our hotel room. We stayed in one room; our parents and two other brothers stayed in another.

Before we left the banquet room, I overheard the escort

tell my father, "You'll stay here tonight. Tomorrow you'll fly to your destination to meet your brother."

My father seemed anxious to get back on an airplane and fly to Nashville right then.

Me? I didn't mind having to spend the night in San Francisco. Not if they planned to keep feeding us like this.

When the escort opened the door to our hotel room, I thought we were at a palace. "Wow, can you believe this place?"

"No," Xay said.

Without a word, Kham Dy jumped into the middle of the king-sized bed and went right to sleep.

"Look, a television," Xay said. Neither of us had seen one up close before. "I wonder how you get it to work."

"Let's find out." I started turning knobs.

"You're going to break it. You should just leave it alone."

"No, I won't. Besides, I once saw a policeman watching Jackie Chan on a television in the security shed at Ban Vinai. Don't you want to watch Jackie Chan?"

"Sure, I guess."

After I turned one or two knobs, the screen lit up and sound came out.

The two of us sat back on the bed and stared in wonder. Unfortunately, it wasn't Jackie Chan.

"What is this?" I said.

"I don't know. It looks like some kind of game, but it's the craziest one I've ever seen."

On the television, oversized men in heavy pads and helmets lined up, then ran into one another.

"Why don't they go around?" I said.

We watched, but neither of us could figure out the point of the game.

After a few minutes, I said, "I'm going to see what else is on."

"No, Xao, don't mess with it. Just leave it here or turn it off."

The Tom Sawyer in me ignored my brother, and I turned knobs until something happened. Somehow, I managed to change the channel.

Instead of athletes, a puppet came on the screen. Apparently he was about to go to bed, just like Xay and me. The puppet walked to the window, shivered, and shut the window.

"Close," he said, then climbed back into bed.

Another puppet came into the room, also dressed for bed, and walked to the window and raised it. "Open."

Then the first puppet shut the window and said, "Close."

The second puppet raised the window again and said, "Open."

The puppets, who called one another Ernie and Bert, gave us our first English lesson. *Sesame Street* sure beat football.

To this day, my brother and I still joke about Bert and Ernie and "open" and "close."

After my brother and I went to bed, I sympathized with Bert. This was my first time sleeping on an actual mattress. The bed was amazing, but neither my brother nor I could figure out how we were supposed to sleep under the sheets. The hotel maid had tucked them in so tightly that we couldn't squeeze between the covers. Instead, we slept on top and shivered all night.

The next morning a shuttle bus arrived to take us back to the airport.

"Next stop: Nashville," my father said.

"And Grandmother?" I replied.

"Yes, and your grandmother." He smiled.

I was so excited that I could hardly contain myself. I did manage to eat breakfast, another meal of firsts, in which I discovered Corn Flakes, bacon, and sausage. I had yet to try a food in America I didn't like.

The plane from San Francisco to Nashville was much smaller than the 747 we'd taken from Bangkok. After everyone had boarded, one of the flight attendants introduced herself. She knew we were moving from the other side of the world to Nashville and was assigned to take special care of us.

I looked up at her in amazement. Tall, blonde, blue-eyed, she looked like an angel. And her nose. I could not stop staring at her nose. All the people I'd known had short or very flat noses, but this woman's was long and shaped just right.

Once the plane was in the air, this flight attendant brought my brothers and me some chocolate milk along with some coloring books and crayons.

I opened the book and laughed. "Xay, remember these guys?" Then I spoke my first English words: "Open, close."

Xay laughed. "Ernie and Bert must be big stars in America. They're everywhere."

Halfway through the flight, I was tired of coloring, so I drew the mountains of Laos with a river flowing down. During my time in school in Ban Vinai, this had been my favorite picture to draw. When I was finished, I gave the page to the flight attendant with the beautiful nose and tried to explain that this was my village where I'd grown up.

Unfortunately, she didn't speak Hmong, Lao, or Thai, and my English was limited to "open" and "close." She smiled and took the picture as if she understood.

From the sky, Nashville looked different from San Francisco. It was October, which meant many of the trees we could see from the air had multicolored leaves: reds, yellows, and oranges. *What amazing trees.*

Once we were finally on the ground, I couldn't wait to get off the plane. An escort led us up the long, narrow hallway and through a door.

Standing there were two of my uncles. I dashed out to hug them and held on for a long time. After they'd left the camp, I'd wondered if I would ever see them again.

"It is so good to see you, my brother," my uncle said to my father.

Both were obviously fighting back tears.

My uncle then led us out of the airport and to a brown Datsun station wagon, the first actual car I would ever ride in.

"Who's car is this?" my father asked.

"Mine. I bought it myself."

Wow, I thought. My *family has always been so poor. Here in America, everyone truly is rich.* I was so proud of my uncle. He had lived in America such a short time and already had made something of himself.

The nine of us crammed into the little Datsun for the drive to my uncle's apartment, our new home. I pressed my face against the window the entire drive. So many cars sped past that I couldn't count them all. And the buildings? Oh, what magnificent buildings! Even the large signs advertising food and everything else fascinated me. *This has to be paradise.*

My uncle exited Interstate 40 and made his way into an apartment complex next to the highway. As we pulled in and slowed to a stop, I beheld the most wonderful sight in the entire world: my grandmother.

I leapt out, ran across the lot, and fell into her arms. As she held me tightly, I sobbed. Soon I felt another set of arms around me as my father embraced his mother. Before I knew it, our entire family had joined in a giant group hug there in the parking lot at 55 Carroll Street.

This must be what heaven's like. It was the moment I'd dreamed of. I never wanted it to end.

20

"I'm All In"

On July 6, 2007, the World Series of Poker had started with 6,358 players. At high noon on Tuesday, July 17, we were down to nine, including me. This was the final table. Whoever went out first would walk away with over $525,000, but no one wants that. Making the final table is the ultimate dream of every poker player, but once you make it, getting there is no longer enough. You want to win.

It's not just the money. The World Series of Poker is like baseball's World Series and football's Super Bowl and all of boxing's championship belts put together. The winner truly is a *world* champion. People from around the globe flock to Vegas to play in this one event. The nine players at this final table alone represented six different countries.

For these reasons, simply sitting at the final table is more pressure than most people can take. Everyone starts off playing even tighter than they have the rest of the tournament.

No one ever goes crazy and goes all in on the first hand. The pressure is too great to do anything so foolish.

Then again, poker is always about pressure, especially to survive. The stakes are not life and death, but they can feel that way with millions in chips in front of you.

No real poker player wants to depend on the luck of the draw to win a hand. You end up losing as often as you win when everything comes down to luck. The key to the game is knowing when to apply pressure to your opponents and to continue until they fold.

You always win when your opponent folds to you, but you never know what may happen when a hand goes to the flop or the turn or all the way to the river card.

During the first round of the final table, the big blinds were 240,000 and the small blinds were set at 120,000 with the antes, or minimum bets, at 30,000. This meant for the first two and a half hours of play, the pot began at 630,000 before anyone did anything.

All of us had begun the tournament with 20,000 in chips. I started play this day in eighth place with 8.45 million.

With my stack size and lack of experience, I looked like the easiest player not only to push around but to shove right out of the tournament. Vegas oddsmakers and most Internet poker sites agreed. They placed the odds of my winning at ten to one, very poor indeed when you consider there were only nine of us left.

I drew the fourth position at the table. Lee Watkinson,

the most successful professional player left in the tournament, sat to my immediate left in seat five. This was his fifth final table at a World Series of Poker event, which is a remarkable achievement. With just under 10 million in chips, however, he was in sixth place and nearly as vulnerable as me. Even so, I regarded him as a dangerous player, perhaps the most dangerous at the final table.

Next to Lee, with over 21 million in chips, was the odds-on favorite to take home the main event championship bracelet: Tuan Lam. Oddsmakers put him at three to one to win.

On Tuan's left, in seventh position with 22 million, was chip leader Philip Hilm of Denmark, a hard-to-read player with a lot of experience. Like Lee Watkinson, he was dangerous, even more so given his huge chip stack.

John Kalmar from England sat in eighth position. His 20 million in chips put him in third place. John was a good player and a very likable guy.

Twenty-two-year-old Hevad Khan, the youngest player at the final table, was in ninth position. The fact that he'd made it this far was surprising since almost all of his poker experience had come from playing online. Just over 800,000 chips separated Hevad, in seventh place, and me. Given the size of the pots at the final table, that difference was nothing.

Raymond Rahme of South Africa, the oldest player still standing, at sixty-two, had the button for the first hand in the first position. This meant he was the last person to have to act in the hand. He started play in fourth place with over 16 million in chips.

The short stack belonged to Alex Kravchenko of Russia, who had 6.57 million in chips. He and I had gone up against one another many times over the past few days, with mixed results.

The last player at the table was another one I was well familiar with. Lee Childs sat to my immediate right. With just over 13 million in chips, he was in fifth place. Lee and I had played many memorable hands during the past few days. I think both of us would have preferred to be seated apart, but the luck of the draw put us side by side. Thankfully, I had the better position. On most hands, I played after him, which gave me a real advantage.

The dealer wished us all good luck before shuffling, and off we went.

I took a deep breath and glanced at my hand. *Just like any other table,* I told myself. *This is just like any other table. Play your game, and play to win.*

After my little pep talk, I looked around the table. Everyone seemed more than a little nervous, which only made sense. All of us were close enough to the title to think we could win it, yet we knew how quickly our chip stacks could shrink to nothing.

No one planned on doing anything crazy. Being the first eliminated would be bad enough; busting out on one of the first few hands would be humiliating.

I couldn't allow the pressure of the moment to intimidate me. Poker is about pressure, and I wouldn't let it stop me. I was under the gun—the first to either call the big blind, raise, or fold—on the first hand, but I refused to act like it in my style of play.

"I raise, 1.4 million." I made the first bet of the final table. Given my chip stack, this was a fairly aggressive play but not crazy.

John Kalmar called, while everyone else folded.

"Two point five million," I said after the flop.

Kalmar immediately folded, and I took the first pot of the final table.

I acted as if I'd done nothing more remarkable than take out the trash at home, but in my mind I was breathing a sigh of relief.

This first pot moved me from next to last place to sixth place. More than that, it made the butterflies in my stomach go away. I knew I could press hard and be successful. At this point, I had no idea how I might finish, but I knew I could play my game. If I busted out, it would be on my terms. I wanted to take the initiative, be the aggressor when I could, and take the tournament to the other players. This approach enabled me to win four of the first eight hands, which shocked the experts and fans but didn't surprise me. I knew I could do this.

The real test, and my tournament so far, would come down to hand nine.

The cards were dealt. Lee Childs, the first to act, raised 720,000, putting the pot at 1.35 million.

I was next. I never look at my cards until all of the players who must act before me have done so. Lee's 720,000 bet was rather aggressive for someone sitting in the first position. That is, he more than doubled the pot without first seeing how anyone else played. That got my attention.

I glanced at Lee. I knew he'd played tight over the first eight hands. For him to make such an aggressive move, he had to be holding some good cards.

I looked at mine for the first time. Pocket jacks, a good hand, but Lee and I had gone up against one another enough times to tell me that he might have something even better. Based on his earlier play, I put him on pocket nines or tens or maybe an ace-king or ace-queen.

All right, Lee, let's see what kind of hand you really have. I did nothing for fifteen seconds. I sat there and counted off the time in my head, just as I did before every bet. On the previous six days of play, I'd waited ten seconds before acting; for the final table, I pushed it to fifteen. I knew right off what I planned to do, but I waited as a way of heightening the emotions of the other players at the table. *Fourteen . . . fifteen.*

"Two point five million."

The other seven players immediately folded, which worked in my favor. If one of the chip leaders had jumped in this hand, they could have pushed me into folding or risking my entire tournament to stay in the pot. Going head-to-head with Lee meant I could be the one to apply the pressure.

My bet did exactly that. To keep playing, Lee had to kick in another 1.78 million. His reaction would show me how good a hand he actually had.

At this point, a player with a high pocket pair typically goes all in and throws the pressure back on the player who raised. Lee didn't. Instead, he called.

Hmmmm, you have a good hand but not a great hand. And

you are afraid I have something even better. Good. That's exactly what I want you to think.

The three flop cards were seven of clubs, four of diamonds, and two of clubs. I had a pretty good idea that these cards did Lee no good, and he probably thought the same thing of my situation. Neither one of us would have been so foolish as to sink over 3 million apiece in a pot with nothing more than pocket sevens or fours or twos.

I wanted him to think I had pocket kings or aces. It was about time to find out if my plan would work.

After the flop, Lee was the first to act. He paused for a few seconds, let out a small sigh, then said, "Three million."

That was exactly what I was waiting for. Lee's bet was conservative, coming in at just under half the pot size. He was playing this hand tight. His wager told me he lacked confidence. It was time to apply the pressure.

Before Lee could move his chips into the center of the table, I announced, "I'm all in."

Lee immediately let out a long breath, which told me, "Mission accomplished."

A couple of days earlier, I had used a similar strategy to force him to fold pocket kings to my queen high. On that hand, I didn't even have a pair. There was no way I could have won that hand if we'd gone all the way to the river, but he folded to me anyway. He'd also made the mistake of showing me his cards after he folded that hand. I learned I could exert enough pressure to get him to fold a superior hand to me, and that was exactly what I was trying to do now.

Lee finished moving his 3 million in chips to the center of the table, let out another long breath, and stood up. He pulled off his sunglasses and paced, trying to figure out what to do next.

My ball cap low, my dark glasses covering my eyes, my hands cupped over my mouth, I didn't move. I sat in the exact same position I did for every hand.

Believe me when I say I don't have a poker face. Not even close. I have to cover as much of myself as possible to even have a chance at the table.

Because he had a slight chip lead on me, Lee could send me home if he called. However, if he called and lost, his stack would be so small that his final table would be as good as over.

I didn't know who had the better hand, but that didn't matter. I wanted him to think I did. I also wanted him to know I was completely committed to this pot. He could not pressure me into folding. If he wanted a chance at the more than 20 million lying on the table, he was going to have to risk his tournament.

Five of the longest minutes of my adult life passed while Lee continued pacing around the room. Once or twice he went near the stands to talk to his father. I couldn't hear their conversations, but when I watched the hand later on ESPN, I discovered his father actually helped me.

Lee said, "I don't know if I can lay it down."

His father replied, "You'll know," which I believe basically meant his father was giving him permission to fold.

If Lee had never gone to his father, I'm sure he would have

called and my tournament would have been over. That's why I say poker is all about applying pressure. That pressure makes people do things they know they shouldn't do, and when you're the one applying it, you usually come out on top.

As all of this played out around me, I sat as still as I could and repeated to myself, *Sit and fold your hand, Lee. Just fold the hand. You can do it. It's easy. Just lay your cards down and say, "I fold."*

After another couple of laps around the room, Lee sat back down, leaned toward me, and said, "Big hand, huh, Jerry?"

His eyes nearly bore a hole through me, but I didn't flinch. If I had, I would've been toast. If he'd watched the bill of my ball cap closely, he would have seen it shaking ever so slightly. I feared he might actually call, and I knew my chances of winning the hand based on luck were not good. I didn't know it at the time, but I had only a 9 percent chance of taking the pot if the hand went all the way to the river. Those are terrible odds. Of course, they were the same odds Vegas had put on my winning the entire tournament.

I didn't say a word as I sat there doing my best imitation of a statue. *Come on, Lee, fold. Fold. Fold. Fold. Just throw down your cards and fold.* My heart beat so loudly in my ears that I could have sworn ESPN's microphones picked up the rhythm and everyone at home could hear it.

After a couple more sighs, Lee said to the other players, "I'm sorry, fellas."

From across the table, Ray Rahme said, "No problem. It's a big call." Ray probably shouldn't have said anything, but the fact that he did played into my strategy. His response to Lee confirmed how much was riding on this hand. No one wanted to go out before the tenth hand. I knew that; Lee knew that; everyone knew that. By speaking up, Ray was in essence saying, "I sure wouldn't want to be in your shoes right now, facing elimination so early at the final table."

The pressure on Lee was enormous.

After what seemed like an eternity, Lee raised his cards in his right hand as if he would fold.

Finally, I thought.

Lee looked at me. "I'm going to show you some respect, Jerry." But he hesitated, continuing to stare at me.

I didn't flinch. I knew if I showed the slightest hint of emotion, he would change his mind and call.

He kept staring at me as if he could read my mind, which is exactly what he was trying to do.

"I think you're, oh, I don't know . . ." Lee sighed.

For a second, I thought he'd changed his mind and was about to call. *Oh no. No, don't call. Fold. Just lay your cards down and fold.*

Finally, he dropped his cards on the table, faceup, surrendering the hand.

I glanced at the cards. Pocket queens. He'd folded pocket queens!

A couple months after the tournament, Lee and I ran into one another at Caesar's Palace. He was gracious and congratulated me on winning the entire tournament. The conversation turned quickly to this hand as he told me he'd believed I had pocket kings, exactly what I'd wanted him to think. By that point, after watching the tourney on television, he knew if he'd called, he might have been where I was now.

But on the day of the tournament, when this hand played out, I couldn't let him know. As I collected my chips, I refused to show the slightest sign of relief.

Lee said, "I know you didn't have me beat," which I took as his request to see my cards.

I never turned them. Even though this hand was over, I wanted to keep the pressure on him.

"I think I made a bad lay down," Lee said to the rest of the players.

"Bad lay down," Ray responded.

Stacking my chips, I didn't say a thing. And what a stack I now had. In one hour, my 8.45 million had grown to over 20 million. Only Tuan Lam and Philip Hilm had more.

Okay, Jerry, keep playing your game, and you will win this thing. No longer did I believe I had a chance to win; I now expected to win. For the first time since play had begun a week and a half before, I knew I would be disappointed if I was not the last man standing.

This hand also placed a little bit of fear in my opponents, who knew I'd do whatever it took to come out on top. As I said, poker is about who can most effectively apply pressure. It's also about who can stand up under it.

I believe every one of us is a prisoner of comfort. We all have our personal comfort zones, and we don't want to leave them. On this hand, I was able to shove Lee out of his and thus get him to make a decision he didn't want to. No matter how much he tried to turn it around on me, I pushed back even harder.

My brain was swirling with all of these thoughts after hand nine, but I couldn't allow it to distract me. As important as this hand was, it was now over. The dealer had already started shuffling the cards.

I didn't know it, but nearly 200 hands of poker and another 15 hours stretched out before me. This marathon was far from over.

21

This Is America?

Our first full day in America, we feasted. To celebrate our arrival, every single one of my relatives who lived in America, some from as far away as Memphis, crammed into the four-bedroom apartment my family now shared with my uncle and his family. Tables, all of them loaded with food, lined the living room from one end to another. Unlike the buffet at the San Francisco airport, this meal held no surprises or firsts. Giant bowls spilled over with fried rice and chicken and all my favorite Hmong dishes. Fruit covered another table, including bananas, mangoes—and what we'd now learned were apples and grapes. To wash it all down, we had ice-cold sodas of every kind.

I took one look at this feast and thought, *I will never have to worry about what I'm going to eat tomorrow. From this day forward, I will never be hungry again.*

Those who have been blessed to have never experienced true hunger cannot appreciate the weight of this moment for me. The cause of my little sister's and baby brother's deaths in Ban Vinai had probably been malnutrition. I myself had suffered from it in Thailand. My stomach had bloated as you would see in news footage of starving children in refugee camps in Third World countries. Going from such despair, such hunger, to this feast in the span of a matter of weeks nearly overwhelmed me.

Nearly, but not quite. I managed to hold myself together long enough to grab a plate and stack it as high as I could. Once it was empty, I filled it up again and again until I couldn't eat another bite. I'd never known how good a full belly could feel.

While we feasted, stories filled the room, leaving everyone laughing one minute and crying the next. My grandmother asked about friends and family she'd left behind at Ban Vinai. Too often those questions were answered with sorrowful news; but then another question led to a funny story, and the mood in the room swung back to joy. The entire night was like this: from tears to laughter and back again, all while stuffing ourselves silly.

Afternoon turned to evening.

My grandmother went into her room and came back dragging three large plastic bags. She called, "Xay, Xao, Kham Dy, come here. I have something for you."

The three of us dropped what we were doing and ran to her.

"As soon as I heard you were coming to America," she said, "I started collecting something for each of you." She reached into a bag and pulled out shirts and pants and shoes for the three of us. My grandmother even had underwear for us. I'd never worn it; no one had back in Laos or in the refugee camps.

I could hardly believe my eyes. One of the bags was filled with clothes for only me. I was still wearing the nice pants and shirt I'd put on the day I'd gotten on the bus to leave Ban Vinai; I had no others. "This is all for me?" I asked.

"Yes, Xao, of course." My grandmother smiled. "Here, try them on."

For the next hour or so, my brothers and I threw on one set of clothes after another. As soon as we put one on, we dashed to the bathroom mirror to look. Then we ran back in the living room for the next set.

After I tried on the last clothes, I looked at all of my new shirts and pants and shoes on the floor and felt like the richest boy in the world. It didn't matter to me that none of my clothes were actually new. Nor did I care that my grandmother had collected them from the donation piles at a nearby church. At that moment, looking at more clothes than I ever knew existed, I was so happy.

The apartment was still filled with family when my brothers and I went to bed, which now was a mattress on the floor. In fact, I wouldn't have an actual bed until I went to college. Even after we would move to Kansas City and later to Fresno, I would sleep on a mattress on the floor. We couldn't afford anything more.

I woke up the next morning to the smells of fried chicken, egg rolls, and pork ribs. What a glorious aroma! We feasted a second day.

Later, in the afternoon, my uncle took the children to the local school to register for classes. Even though we didn't speak English, my father wanted us to start school as soon as possible. I had excelled in school in Ban Vinai and was probably at the top of my class there.

However, Nashville was not Ban Vinai. Not knowing the language meant I had to start at the bottom. Actually, I had to start below the bottom. Back in Thailand, I had completed fifth grade and was now ready for sixth. Yet because I was so small, the school officials in Nashville put me all the way back in fourth grade. Even then, most of the kids were taller than me.

Once school started, my brothers and I spent most of our days in the English as a second language classes. Outside of that class, I quickly realized I now lived in a different world than the one I'd imagined.

My Hmong name, Xao, is pronounced "so." The kids made fun of me, calling me "So what?"

One skinny kid named Curtis particularly disliked me and tried to pick a fight every single day, calling me "Ching Chong" and "Chink." I had no idea what he was saying until one of my cousins explained it. Curtis loved the fact that I was smaller than him. He bullied me and all the other smaller children. He thought I was the stupidest kid in the world because my English was so bad. I would not miss him when my family would move to Kansas City at the end of the school year.

While we children went to school, my father went out and found a job. Even though he couldn't speak any English, not even "open" and "close," he soon found a job at the local Gibson

Guitar factory, where my uncle also worked.

Even though he earned only minimum wage, my father took great pride in his work. His boss put him in charge of polishing the guitars as they reached the end of the assembly line. He put his all into it. At the end of the day, he dragged himself into our home, totally exhausted.

Few men would swallow their pride and take such menial work. My father, the army captain, pastor, and village leader who'd saved his people from certain death, never thought twice about it.

To us, he was the most respected man on earth. To the other workers at the Gibson Guitar factory, he was just another immigrant worker who couldn't speak the language. Though my father spoke three languages fluently, unfortunately English was not one of them, and his coworkers never let him forget it.

One day during their lunch break, my father and uncle went to put some sugar in their coffee. The sugar packets sat next to salt packets. My father, not able to distinguish one from the other, grabbed one packet, tore it open, and poured the contents into his coffee.

Off to the side, his American coworkers watched. As soon as my father took a drink, they fell over laughing. He'd chosen the wrong one.

My father dismissed himself, went outside, found a secluded spot, and wept. But he never let his coworkers know this event had bothered him in the least. He simply went back to work, polishing guitars with the same pride he'd once put into our fields.

The cruelty of a few was more than offset by the kindness of others. A local Church of Christ went out of their way to help Hmong families. We went to the church every Sunday even though we didn't understand English and Pastor A.T. Pate didn't speak a word of Hmong.

One Sunday we found a way to overcome the language barrier. The church started singing "Jesus Loves Me."

All of the Hmong in the auditorium immediately recognized the tune. In Laos, we always stood for this song, so we all jumped to our feet and began singing in Hmong.

The English-speaking part of the crowd turned toward us and stood up as well.

Everyone smiled and laughed and celebrated while we sang "Jesus Loves Me" in two languages. In that moment, I felt like we all belonged there together. The cultural barrier didn't really matter since Jesus loved us all.

The church had a program teaching English to the Hmong in the evenings. Even though I was in the ESL classes at school, I went to the church classes as well. At twelve years old, I didn't care much for the fourth grade. I wanted to learn English and get in the right grade as quickly as I could. The Thai school in Ban Vinai had put me on a middle school level in math and science. Once I learned English, I could be on my way back up.

I didn't just attend the church; my father taught me the importance of work and repaying the kindnesses others extended to me. After classes, I volunteered for whatever needed to be done around the church.

One Saturday morning, after I'd helped Pastor Pate stack chairs, he asked, "Xao, are you hungry?"

I spoke enough English to understand. "Yes, sir. A little bit."

"So am I. Let's go get a couple of hot dogs. I know the best place in Nashville for dogs. My treat."

"Okay," I said, but inside I kept wondering, *Hot dog? They don't eat dogs in America. Is my pastor making fun of me? Does he think my family eats dogs? I just spent my morning helping him stack chairs, and this is the thanks I get? I thought he was my friend.*

I climbed in his truck and rode a few blocks from the church.

"This is the spot," Pastor Pate said. "Best hot dogs in town." He pulled into a shopping center, then led me to a stand in front of one of the stores.

If he had looked closely at me and read my mind, he would have known I was anything but thrilled about eating dog meat.

"Two dogs with everything," he said to the man in the white apron.

I studied the stand. The familiar sights of mustard, ketchup, onions, and sauerkraut made me feel a little better. Then I watched as the man placed what looked like sausages on the buns.

It doesn't look like dog to me. Still, I was more than a little nervous. I thought perhaps they'd used dog to make the sausages.

"Here you go, Xao," Pastor Pate said. "Have you ever had one?"

"No, sir."

"Then you're in for a treat."

I waited until he'd taken a bite before I tried my hot dog.

When I took that first bite, I thought, *Wow! I hope this isn't really dog meat, because it is really good.*

Later that night when I got home, one of my cousins explained hot dogs to me. I couldn't wait to have another, especially now that I knew no dogs were harmed in making them.

A few months after we arrived in America, more of our family came to Nashville from Ban Vinai. All the relatives returned to the apartment and threw a huge party. The new arrivals moved in with us.

A newspaper reporter showed up at the apartment a short time later. The reporter had heard that thirty-eight people were all living in a small, four-bedroom apartment in the Nashville projects.

I didn't know what "projects" were, but I had done a head count and, sure enough, there were thirty-eight of us. My mother and father had one bedroom, and my uncle and his children had another. Another uncle and his family had the other room. My uncle's son-in-law had moved in, and a widowed aunt from Thailand and her daughter were also there. Some people slept in the living room on the sofa bed. The rest of us slept on mattresses on the floor.

None of the adults thought too much of the situation. I'm sure they would have liked to have more room, but in this strange new land, we found safety in numbers.

Later, I would ask my father why so many of us had lived in such a small space.

"None of us knew how to find a place of our own," my father

would tell me. "When my uncle first came to Nashville, his American sponsor had already found this place for him. We didn't know how to go house hunting in America. Back in Laos, we just went out into the jungle, cut down some trees, and built whatever kind of house we wanted. But we weren't in Laos anymore."

The reality of our situation didn't hit me until one Sunday afternoon when our pastor took my brother and me to dinner at his house.

Pastor Pate's car, a Cadillac, felt luxurious. I nudged Xay. "Can you believe this car?" I whispered. "It's sooooo big."

Xay nodded.

I watched out the window as we drove a series of tree-lined streets. They looked nothing like the freeway right outside our door. We had a few trees on the apartment grounds, but they didn't look healthy.

The pastor turned onto his street. All of the lawns were so green and lush. In the projects, what little grass we had between buildings had been trampled; the lawn there was more like dirt and pavement. Our pastor's driveway, curving around like a small street, didn't look like any driveway I'd ever seen. To be honest, I hadn't seen many.

The house itself was spectacular. Inside, the living room had a nice sofa and chairs. In our apartment, we had an old sofa; you had to watch where you sat or the springs would stick you in the rear end. We also had an old chair, but the fabric on the arms had long since frayed away.

At our pastor's home, everything was nice. From the carpets to the drapes to the furniture, it was like nothing I had ever seen. And it felt so big, much bigger than our apartment, though only five people lived here.

And then we ate dinner. The quality of the ingredients was better than what we ate every day. They even served the meal on real china, not the plastic plates and cups we used.

After dinner, we went to the basement, where there was a Ping-Pong table.

"Do you boys play?" Pastor Pate asked.

"Yes," I said. I'd played in Thailand and loved it.

"Good. Let's play."

He served the ball toward me. I think he was trying to take it easy on me since I was such a small boy. However, he hit the ball in such a way that it bounced kind of high on my side. I spiked it so hard he hardly saw it fly past.

"You have played." He laughed.

I now understand that the Pates were not rich by American standards but led a normal, middle-class life. At that time, though, seeing their house changed the way I saw our way of life. Till now, I'd seen everything in America in light of where we'd come from. Our apartment may have been crammed with people, but it sure beat Ban Vinai. Now I saw my life in terms of what America had to offer.

When Pastor Pate drove us home and let us out in front of our apartment, I took a close look around the neighborhood. Graffiti covered some of the walls. Broken-down cars and trash littered the streets. A dilapidated fence separated our apartment complex from the interstate.

A rusted pedestrian bridge crossed above the highway. As I looked at it now, I realized it was not safe. Everyone in the projects had to walk on it, but we were probably taking our lives in our own hands when we did.

Our neighborhood wasn't safe either. There was a reason my parents insisted all of us stay inside after dark, and it wasn't merely our early bedtimes. After years of having bombs blow up just over the next hill back home, I'd always ignored the violence here in our neighborhood.

I now realized everyone in America didn't live like this.

That night, lying on my mattress on the floor next to my brothers, I thought, *You know what? Poverty exists everywhere. Even in America.*

The thought made me a little sad, until I also realized something else about my new home. Yes, we were poor by American standards, but I also knew this country presented an incredible opportunity even to someone like me who was just beginning to learn the language and customs.

Just as in the hills of Laos, no one was going to hand anything to me here. *But if I work hard enough,* I thought, *anything is possible here.* We hadn't come for handouts. We'd come for the opportunity only America could offer.

That revelation changed my life. I'm thankful it came soon enough for me to do something with it.

22
The Jerry Yang Show

When play began at the final table, I was in eighth place. After my all-in gamble on the ninth hand, I'd jumped up to third. Philip Hilm still had the chip lead, with 23 million in chips. I'd watched Philip the past couple of days and noticed he liked to be the aggressor at the table, taking the initiative and forcing others to play his game.

Throughout day six, I had watched Philip bully one player after another.

A few hadn't given in to his pressure, and I was grateful for their persistence. When they'd forced him to go all the way to the river, I could see the kinds of hands he played.

Tight players will only go into a pot with a pocket pair or a pocket hand with at least a 30 percent chance of winning. However, on day six especially, Philip had consistently played hands like eight-five off suit, or seven-four off suit, hands with a less than one-half percent chance of taking down a pot.

Most players won't play these hands because even if they pair the eight or five, anything from a pair of aces on down to nines or sixes will beat them. On top of that, hitting a straight or a flush from such a hand is next to impossible.

Yet Philip Hilm had played them quite effectively.

I knew if I were to have any kind of chance against Philip Hilm, I'd have to be even more aggressive than he was. Aggressive but not reckless. When I drew a strong hand, I would push hard to see if he would push back.

Hand fourteen gave me the opportunity I was looking for.

I was next to last to act before the blinds. Everyone folded around the table to me. I looked at my cards. Pocket eights, a strong hand that prevails more than 50 percent of the time.

I counted off fifteen seconds in my head and then announced, "Two point five million."

An opening bet of this size, ten times the big blind, qualified as aggressive. Very aggressive. In fact, a few so-called experts later called my moves like this reckless, a sign of an amateur.

Nothing could be further from the truth. My strategy for Philip Hilm dictated making a bet big enough to scare off the next two players yet small enough to entice him to stay in the hand.

It worked.

Lee Watkinson immediately folded, as did Tuan Lam in the small blind.

Philip Hilm smiled at me. "Big raise, Jerry." He looked at his cards and thought for a moment. "I call."

That was exactly what I'd wanted him to do: call, not raise. I certainly didn't want him to play even more aggressively than I was and go all in. I don't think I could have put my tournament on the line with pocket eights before the flop. Too many cards could still beat me.

By calling, Philip left the door open to me to dictate the style of play the rest of the hand.

The flop came: ace, ten, and the sweetest-looking little eight in the whole wide world.

Philip, the first to act, checked. His check may have been an attempt to lure me into a trap, but I didn't think so. I knew if he had pocket aces or tens, or even ace-ten, he would have pushed hard.

Now it was my turn to push. "Three million."

Philip stared a hole into me. "Call."

The turn came: a three of diamonds.

Philip checked again.

The mix of suits on the board meant a flush was highly unlikely, not that it mattered. Philip hadn't played as if he was working on a flush. While a gut shot straight still loomed, the odds were stacked against it.

Barring a bad card on the river, I knew I had him. "All in."

He had more than enough chips to cover me, which meant I would go home if I lost this hand, but my chip stack was close enough to his to make sure that if Philip called and lost, his tournament would be all but over. Based on what was already on the board, I didn't think he would call.

"Good hand, Jerry," Philip said as he slid his cards toward the dealer, folding the hand and giving me the 11.39 million in the pot.

After less than an hour and a half of play, I was now chip leader at the final table of the main event of the World Series of Poker with over 25.04 million in chips.

As I stacked the chips, John Kalmar looked across the table and said with a smile, "Tell you what, Jerry. I'm just going to sit here and let you get everybody else's chips, and then battle it out head-to-head. How's that sound?"

I have to say, it sounded pretty good to me.

Then Hevad Khan spoke up. "I told you since day one: best player I've ever played with in my life."

"Thank you." I appreciated his compliment, even though I knew it was far from true. However, these comments helped me in another way. Just as Kenny Tran had tried to knock me off my game by making derogatory comments at the beginning of day six, these two well-meant comments were actually unintentional insults to the more experienced players still at the table. Essentially, John and Hevad were challenging the top players to step up to the plate and do something before this psychologist from California stole the main event bracelet right out from under their noses.

One of the best players accepted that challenge on the very next hand.

Many times, after losing a big hand, a player immediately wants to get his chips back. And when he has the chance to retake them from the player who just beat him, that can be hard to resist.

Hand fifteen came. The first few players all folded.

When it was my time to act, I looked at an ace-king off suit, also known as a big slick. "One million." While not as aggressive as the one for the previous hand, this too was a very strong bet.

Watkinson and Lam folded. Now it was Philip Hilm's turn to act. He called.

Both blinds folded. Once again, it was me against Philip Hilm.

The flop hit the table. It was a king of diamonds, a jack of diamonds, and a five of clubs, giving me a pair of kings with a strong kicker. The two diamonds made a flush possible if he was holding diamonds.

Just as in the previous hand, Philip checked.

"Two million," I said.

Philip called.

The dealer laid down the turn card, a two of hearts, a card that could not have helped either of us unless Philip was playing a pair of twos, which I highly doubted.

Philip checked to me once more.

I had the hammer and decided to use it. "Four million."

Now it was Philip Hilm's chance to be the aggressor. He watched me push my chips into the middle. Then he sniffed and said, "I'm all in."

Believe it or not, the past couple of days I'd noticed every time Hilm bluffed, he'd sniffed. Now I had to decide whether he was sniffing because he was bluffing or because the air-conditioning was making his nose run.

I breathed out. It was time for me to learn if all my research, notes, and read of the table were right or wrong. "I call."

Hilm smiled at me and flipped his cards over. My research had paid off. He had an eight-five, both diamonds, the same kind of hand he'd played the day before when he'd pushed around the short stacks.

Yeah! I screamed inside. Outwardly, I showed nothing.

When he saw my big slick, Philip groaned. Although he still had a chance of making the flush or hitting another five, I held the advantage. He had to get very lucky on the river, or his day was over.

A six of clubs hit the table for the river, and just like that Philip Hilm went from chip leader to the first man out, all in the span of one hour and twenty-eight minutes.

After taking all of Philip's chips in two hands, I now held a commanding chip lead with twice as many chips as anyone else. Before I let that go to my head, I looked at Philip Hilm, shook hands with the other players at the table, and wished each one luck as Philip headed toward the door.

At one time, he looked unbeatable, too, I reminded myself.

Half an hour later, in hand twenty-one, I found myself in another head-to-head showdown with the second of the three most dangerous players at the final table. I was in the small blind; Lee Watkinson, the most accomplished pro at the table, had the big blind. All the other players had folded their way around to us.

I raised a million.

Lee paused, then said, "All in."

The previous two years, Lee Watkinson had been one of my favorite players to watch. He's what I call tight-aggressive. That means he doesn't play many hands, but when he has the cards, he pushes hard. The only way to have a chance against a player like this is to be the opposite. You must push when they are tight and be cautious when they become the aggressor.

Lee had basically treaded water the first nearly two hours of play. This was his first all in, which made me cautious.

Then I thought back on the reams of notes I had on him. *This doesn't make any sense. He doesn't usually play like this. If he had pocket aces or kings, he would have slow played and kept me in the hand to milk me for everything he could get. No, this looks like a classic case of a frustrated player trying to scare everyone out of the hand early so he can grab the blinds and antes.*

I looked closely at Lee and tried to figure out what he was holding. *He has to have something big enough to survive a call, maybe ace-five or a small pair, but I don't think he has the hammer he wants me to think he has.*

All of this went through my head in about two seconds.

"How many chips does he have?" I asked the dealer. The time it took them to count gave me a little more time to make a decision. I knew I had a decent hand: ace-nine off suit, and I put my odds of winning the hand at about fifty-fifty.

It turned out he had 9.745 million in chips; I had 45.09 million. With my chip lead, fifty-fifty odds were good enough. "I call."

We turned our cards. When I saw Lee's ace-seven off suit, I pumped my fist. Only three cards in the deck could beat me, barring some miraculous flush draw.

As we waited for the flop, turn, and river, I did what I always do when a big pot is on the line. I prayed.

ESPN's cameras and microphones focused on me asking God to glorify His name. Only later, when I watched the broadcast at home, did I see Lee's fiancée, Timmie, sitting in the stands, praying just as hard. Most television viewers probably found this odd; no one tuning in to a poker match expects to see a prayer meeting break out!

Thankfully, I took the hand. Lee Watkinson's day was over. In an interview several months later, Timmie was quoted as saying, "I guess you just can't outpray Jerry Yang."

I don't think that's the case. However, God was gracious to me that day. In two hours, I'd knocked out two of the players I feared most and, as a result, increased my chip stack from 8.45 million to a staggering 55 million.

Seven hands later, I knocked out Lee Childs, giving me over half of all the chips in play.

In less than three hours, I'd personally knocked out three of the best players at the table and taken a commanding chip lead. Never in my wildest dreams could I have envisioned this day turning out like this.

When I watched the ESPN broadcast, I heard Norman Chad refer to the final table as "The Jerry Yang Show" after I knocked out Hevad Khan in hand fifty-six.

ESPN edits the action so much that it looked as if I'd taken out four players in about an hour. Even so, five hours at the final table is a short time. To those watching at home, and even in the stands in the Amazon Room, a victory for me now looked inevitable.

I knew better. Raymond Rahme took out John Kalmar, which left three large obstacles standing between me and the main event bracelet: Rahme, Tuan Lam, and, of course, the formidable Alex Kravchenko.

Of all the players, the most surprising one to still be at the table, besides me, had to be Alex Kravchenko. That is not to take anything away from Alex. He's an incredible player, but he'd spent most of day six stuck on the short stack, which is where he was now.

With his just over 6 million in chips at the start of the day, most people thought he would be the first one out. I knew better. Alex is an excellent poker player. Whereas Philip Hilm played aggressively throughout the tournament, Alex was the opposite. I knew anytime he jumped into a pot, he had a hand.

They say Texas Hold 'Em is a marathon, the proverbial tortoise and the hare kind of race. If that is true, Alex Kravchenko could teach all the tortoises out there a few things.

When you have the short stack, you must be disciplined and wisely choose the hands you'll play. I've rarely witnessed any player execute this strategy with the precision Alex demonstrated at the final table. He picked just the right spots to make an aggressive bet or go all in. Usually everyone folded to him, giving him the blinds and antes. You can survive a long time in a poker tournament if you pick up enough blinds and antes.

During the first five hours of play, only one player, Hevad Khan, actually called him. By the time the river hit the table,

Khan had doubled Alex up and weakened his own tournament.

A short time later, Khan was gone while Alex kept on playing.

I doubled Alex up for the first time just after five in the evening on the fifty-eighth hand. He went all in from the small blind, and I called from the large. I knew I had to knock him out as quickly as possible. I thought my jack-ten off suit gave me my chance.

I was wrong.

He turned over ace-ten off suit and increased his chip stack to just under 10 million, thanks to me.

I still had over 68 million, but that wasn't the point. I'd wanted to knock Alex out. The longer he stuck around, the more dangerous he became.

Going up against a disciplined player demands extreme patience. His strategy relies on his ability to frustrate his opponent into playing borderline hands he can easily beat. A player like Alex Kravchenko refuses to be bullied by the larger stack. The only way to beat him is to wait for him to go all in and call with a superior hand. While that may seem obvious, it's much easier said than done.

In the next eight hours, I doubled up Kravchenko two more times. In the process, my chip stack shrank from a high of over 70 million down to just over 41 million.

I still had the lead but not by much.

The clock pushed toward one in the morning. We had now been playing poker for nearly thirteen hours, with periodic twenty-minute breaks sprinkled in every couple of hours.

In the late afternoon, it had appeared I would make short

work of this final table and easily take home the $8.25 million first prize, but nothing comes easily in this game, especially not with a man like Alex Kravchenko standing in your way.

Hand 167 began with me in the big blind, Alex Kravchenko in the small blind. Tuan Lam, the first to act, folded, as did Raymond Rahme. Alex barely looked at his cards, then slid 2.1 million into the pot.

I looked at my cards. Pocket eights, a hand that has been especially good to me. I glanced at Alex. His raise of 2.1 million was not as aggressive as it would have been twelve hours earlier when the blinds were much lower. He raised by the standard amount, three times the big blind of 600,000. Since he already had 300,000 in the pot, his bet was not that aggressive at all.

My strategy going into the final table was to pick a spot early on and push Alex out of the tournament. I'd tried three times to knock him out and failed, though I still held a two to one lead over him. The three times I'd doubled him up, my hand had been good but not quite good enough.

This seemed like the perfect spot to turn the tables. *Come on, pocket eights, don't fail me now.* I swept my hand above my chips and announced, "I'm all in."

Alex didn't look at me. He stared at his chip stack for a moment, thinking. Many players will look at their cards or stand up and walk around the room nervously while trying to decide whether or not to put their tournament on the line. Not Alex. He sat there, thinking, then said calmly, "I call."

The crowd in the Amazon Room came alive. Raymond

Rahme jumped up and said something like, "Why'd he call? Why'd he call?"

Alex showed the same steely discipline he had throughout the tournament. He stood up and turned his cards. Ace-king off suit. Ace-king, aka, a big slick, is the fifth strongest hand you can draw in No Limit Texas Hold 'Em. My pocket eights are only the thirteenth strongest. He'd made a very good call. I had come to expect no less from Alex Kravchenko.

Now everything came down to the luck of the draw. I felt confident. In Asian culture, eight is the luckiest number of all. Two eights are even better.

The moment the flop hit the table, I knew I had him. Queen, nine, and . . . you guessed it. An eight.

The only way he could beat me now would be to hit a straight. He needed a jack and a ten on the turn and river, which was a long shot.

I raised my arms and cheered. Unable to stay in one place, I turned around and ran to my cheering section, my family. My brother-in-law happened to be the first person I saw, so I hugged him.

I quickly regained my composure and walked back to the table. "Come on," I said under my breath. "Come on, nothing funny."

The turn card was a four of clubs. The river card didn't matter.

Finally, after thirteen hours, I'd knocked out the most tenacious player in the World Series of Poker.

In hand 169, Raymond Rahme busted out when my ace-five beat his pair of kings.

Now it was down to two, Tuan Lam and me.

The day before the final table, Vegas oddsmakers had made Tuan Lam the odds-on favorite to win the title, while I was the longest of long shots. However, those odds were the exact opposite now.

With 23 million, Tuan had slightly more chips than he'd had at the start of the day. I was leading with over 104 million and had become the first person in the history of the main event to hit the 100 million mark.

However, if I've learned one thing in poker, it's that no lead is ever safe.

Ever.

23

Reaching for the American Dream

My father approached me with a simple request when I was in ninth grade. We'd moved from the projects of Nashville to the projects of Kansas City a couple years earlier. "Xao, please, I ask one thing of you." He looked extremely tired after having spent a long day making tool belts at a leather factory on the other side of the state line in Kansas City, Missouri.

Looking into his eyes that day, I could see that the years of backbreaking work had taken their toll on him, and I felt fortunate that we lived in America. Few men lived to my father's age in our homeland in the hills of Laos.

"What is it, Father?"

"Please finish your education. Graduate from high school. Then you will make your father very proud and happy."

My heart sank.

It wasn't that I thought he'd asked too much of me. No, deep in my heart I knew my father had asked too little. *Have I shown you I'm capable of so little?* I did not dare say it.

Even though his request saddened me, I knew my father had not disrespected me. Over the first fourteen years of my life, I had disrespected myself. It wasn't that I'd struggled academically. From my earliest days in school in Thailand, academics had always come easily to me. Unfortunately, I hadn't yet learned to apply myself. I still wanted to be that Hmong Tom Sawyer and constantly found ways to get into mischief.

I knew hard work and determination alone could lift me out of poverty, but I had to prove my Tom Sawyer days were past.

In Nashville, my full Tom Sawyer had come roaring out one day. One of my cousins owned a bicycle that I absolutely loved, even though it was a girl's. It had the long banana seat, small front tire, and sloping lines like a motorcycle's. My father couldn't afford anything like it, and I didn't have any way to earn money to buy one.

One afternoon, I walked to my cousin's apartment and borrowed the bike, but I'm not sure her family knew that. If we hadn't been related, someone might have accused me of stealing it. I didn't think of it as stealing, though, since I planned to bring it back as good as new.

There was one problem: I could barely ride. I took off on the bike, but I had trouble keeping it upright. Before I knew it—*crash*—I fell on the sidewalk.

I jumped right up and took off again. I got a little farther this time before—*crash*—over I went once again.

After a little while, I managed to keep from falling, which

made me so happy that I pedaled harder. Only then did I discover another difficult part of riding: turning. Instead of falling, this time I crashed right into a tree, the impact throwing me to one side.

Thankfully, I didn't land on anything vital. Maybe on my head, but I wasn't really using it right then, so it didn't matter.

I picked myself up, walked to the bike next to the tree, and planned to take off once again. Whenever I set my mind to learn something, I don't let up until I master it; I still had a lot of work to do with the bicycle.

My life as the Hmong Tom Sawyer always landed me in trouble. And this day was no exception. I picked up my cousin's beautiful new bike only to discover the front wheel looked more like a pretzel.

Oh no! I started to panic but calmed myself. *Just fix it, Xao, and no one will know.*

I looked around until I found two large rocks. After laying the bike sideways, I hammered away at the wheel. Once I'd made it as straight as I could, I snuck the bicycle back to my cousin's apartment and placed it where I'd found it; then I slipped away and hoped no one would notice.

I got caught, of course, but my uncle was very kind, and I didn't get into trouble. Perhaps my uncle had once been a little Tom Sawyer himself.

We may have moved from Nashville to Kansas City, but the Tom Sawyer in me was just as strong as ever. Here I was at the beginning of my freshman year of high school, still trying to squeeze all the fun out of life without ever taking it seriously, and my father was pleading with me, tears in his eyes, to meet such a small goal: to finish high school.

Oh, Father, I am capable of so much more, I thought. *And before I'm finished, I will prove that to you.*

My inner Tom Sawyer died that day, put to death by me. I had no choice. My father saw great potential in me. All he really wanted was for me to have a better life than the one he, an immigrant who couldn't speak English, could give us.

I knew how hard he worked. Every night when he came home, I removed his shoes to show my gratitude for all he'd done for me. "Yes, Father," I said. "I will not let you down. I will finish high school. You'll see."

After my sophomore year, our family moved once again. By this point I had a new sister, Shirley, the first American citizen in my family. Not long after we'd moved to California, my mother had also given birth to another son, Reagan, named after President Ronald Reagan. My parents wanted to move our whole family away from the violence of the projects, and more than that my father wanted to farm again.

I had visions of the slash-and-burn farming we'd done in Laos, performing every task by hand. When we ended up moving near Fresno, though, I quickly discovered that farming in the California's Central Valley is very different.

My father rented a piece of ground, where he grew cherry tomatoes. My brothers and I worked the farm with my father in the afternoons after school and all through the summer.

Even though we didn't have to chop trees by hand and clear a spot on a side of a mountain, as we had in Laos, raising cherry tomatoes was labor intensive. Once they were on the vine, we had to pick them every day.

Did I mention how hot it is in Fresno in the summertime? The temperature climbs into triple digits almost as soon as the sun comes up over the mountains. I thought I might dry up and blow away picking those tomatoes.

When my father later rented his own farm, we also grew green beans, cucumbers, jalapeño peppers, and strawberries. I learned that if you can get water to the plant, anything will grow in California's Central Valley.

I took my promise to my father seriously.

During my freshman year of high school in Kansas City, I had brought home only one B on my report card; the rest were A's.

My sophomore year, I went to Hoover High School in Fresno, where I excelled in everything except English. I tested out of math classes all the way up to trigonometry. The math teacher, Haig Shekerjian, even let me grade papers for his algebra classes. Soon I worked as a tutor with his struggling students. Not only was I excelling in school, but I actually began to enjoy it.

At the end of my sophomore year, I brought home a perfect 4.0 grade point average.

My father noticed. He encouraged me, pushing me to work even harder.

He also worked harder on the farm to try to save money

to put toward college for me. No one can save money like my father can. Even though he worked mainly minimum wage jobs, he'd saved enough to pay cash for a car of his own. Now he had a bigger goal in mind, both for himself and for me.

My father now knew that merely finishing high school was not nearly a lofty enough goal for his second son.

In school, I ran into one problem: my name. No one could pronounce it. When the teachers called roll the first day, they'd come to my name near the end of the list and not know what to say. Sometimes teachers pronounced my first name as "Cho" or "Zo" or "Zou." Even after I corrected them, it took weeks for them to get it right.

My brother had the same problem, so we both decided we needed American names.

For Xay, the choice was easy. He loved Jackie Chan movies even more than I did. The moment he decided to Americanize his name, he became Jackie. (Later, when he would become an American citizen in 1999, he would once again change his name, this time to Jonah. I guess he outgrew his inner Jackie Chan just as I outgrew my inner Tom Sawyer.)

For me, the choice was not so easy.

I wanted to pick a good, strong name. I thought about the name Charlie, but I didn't want to be called Chuck. I also considered the name Michael, like the archangel, but it didn't seem to fit me. I really liked the name John and almost settled on it, till one day while reading the Bible, I found myself staring at the fourth book of the New Testament, John, and thought, *I could never live up to a name like this.*

I also pondered the name Tom. I liked it because I liked Thomas Jefferson. How much more American could you get than that? But I was hesitant to pick it, too, because I of the whole Hmong Tom Sawyer thing.

Tom didn't feel right any more than Charlie or Michael or John did.

All of a sudden, it hit me. I knew the perfect name.

When I first came to America and couldn't speak English, I still liked to watch television, especially cartoons. I didn't need to understand English to enjoy my favorite cartoon, *Tom and Jerry.* I especially liked Jerry the mouse; he reminded me of me. He was so small that everyone always underestimated him. And, like me, he had to scramble for food just to survive. But no matter what challenges he faced, he always came out on top. That big old cat Tom did everything he could to catch him, but nothing worked. Jerry was too smart for him.

That's me, I thought. *Struggle, struggle, struggle. But in the end, Jerry always wins by the sheer force of his determination. I want to be a winner. My name is Jerry.*

I thought no one could possibly come up with a way to make fun of my new name. I was wrong.

One wise guy at my high school called me "Jerry Coke," like Cherry Coke.

I let it get under my skin until an idea hit me.

The next time I saw him, he said, "How's it going, Jerry Coke?"

"Just great, Johnny Pepsi."

He laughed.

We would call each other by these names through high school.

I'd begun attending a Bible study at an Asian Seventh-Day Adventist church after we'd moved to Fresno. Some weeks I also attended church there on Saturdays, in addition to attending church with my family on Sundays. The church sponsored a Christian high school.

After my sophomore year at Hoover, the pastor, Chris Ishii, said, "Jerry, how would you like to go to our Adventist Academy?"

I liked the idea of spending my day in a Christian environment. The school was also much smaller than Hoover High. Like everything else in my life, though, one big obstacle stood in my way: money. My parents couldn't afford to send me to a private school.

"I will pray about it," I told Pastor Ishii.

I did pray, but it seemed impossible. At the public school, I qualified for the low-income lunch program and could ride the bus. With a private school, in addition to the $460 monthly tuition, I had to pay for my own books, field trips, lunch, and transportation.

I called Pastor Ishii. "As much as I would like to go to your school, I simply don't have the money."

"Jerry, if you really want to come, we can find a way. Let's pray about it." Then he said, "Would you be willing to work to help pay your way?"

"Of course." I have never been afraid of hard work.

Pastor Ishii also asked about my grades. When I told him I was a 4.0 student, he said he would get back with me soon.

Two weeks later, he called. "A lady in our church, Mrs. Einhart, owns a nursing home in downtown Fresno and has agreed to help you pay your tuition. However, you'll have to pay for your own books and transportation."

I was overwhelmed. How I would pay for everything else, I didn't know, but I figured I could find a way.

That's when Pastor Ishii surprised me with another bit of news: Mrs. Einhart had offered me a job on the janitorial staff at her nursing home.

Two days later, I finally got to meet the woman who had offered to do something so nice for me.

Mrs. Einhart sat me down. "Jerry, I will do this for you but only on one condition."

"Yes, ma'am?" I had no idea what she'd say next.

"I will help pay your tuition if you give me your word that someday, when you are able, you will show the same kindness to others that I have shown to you."

"Oh, yes, ma'am. I would be honored to do that. I give you my word. I will."

With tuition and book money covered, I only needed transportation.

I talked to my family, and my uncle made me an offer. This was the same uncle who had picked us up at the airport in Nashville. He now lived in Fresno with his family as well.

"Xao, I want you to use my car. You'll have to pay for the insurance and gas, but that's it. It's yours for as long as you need it. Once you're through with it, just give it back."

With that, he handed me the keys to the little brown Datsun station wagon, the very one he'd used to pick us up from the airport when we'd arrived in America five years before.

What more could a young man have asked for?

The next two years, I got up every morning at two o'clock. I worked from three until half past seven sweeping and mopping and vacuuming at Mrs. Einhart's nursing home. After work, I quickly showered, dressed, and drove to school. In the afternoon, I studied and studied. I went to bed by nine o'clock and started the whole thing again early the next morning.

Occasionally I helped out at my father's farm, but he didn't want me there during the school year.

"Go study, Xao. Concentrate on your schoolwork. That's more important than this."

Needless to say, I didn't have much of a social life my last two years of high school. In the end, it was worth it. Not only did I graduate, but I finished at the top of my class.

The day I went to tell my father I was named valedictorian, I could hardly get the words out. "Father, when we came to America, I didn't know a word of English. I struggled early on. But you taught me to work hard, and I have. I did anything and everything I could to become a better student, and it paid off. Father, I will graduate number one in my class, the top student, the valedictorian." My tears poured down.

My father couldn't help himself and cried as well. He

wrapped his arms around me and said, "Son, you have done very well. I am proud of you."

That, more than anything, was my ultimate goal.

After high school, I would go on to Pacific Union College on a full scholarship. The day I told my father I was planning to major in biology and go on to medical school, he nearly burst with pride. When I graduated from high school, he slaughtered a pig and held a giant celebration. The day I graduated from college, he slaughtered a bull and threw an even bigger party.

I was accepted to eight different medical schools, finally deciding on Loma Linda in Southern California. After working so hard through both high school and college, though, I was more than a little burned out.

I deferred medical school one year and took master's level classes at Loma Linda in health psychology. The only reason I'd wanted to be a doctor was to help people in places like the ones where I'd grown up. I discovered I could do the same thing through health psychology.

Breaking this news to my father was one of the hardest things I ever did. The man who had at one time asked only that I finish high school looked at me as if I'd let him down. Even so, the day I received my master's degree, he threw the biggest party yet. Even General Vang Pao came and celebrated with us.

I stayed in school beyond my master's and worked toward my PhD. This time, money didn't get in the way. Something far more important did.

During a Hmong New Year celebration, I met the most

beautiful woman I'd ever seen. We soon married and started a family of our own. I dropped out of graduate school, though I needed only to write my dissertation to finish my doctorate.

My father says to me to this day, "Jerry, all I ask of you is that you finish your doctorate, and I will be happy."

I laugh every time he says it. But never in front of him.

Sue and I settled into a normal American life, complete with car payments and a mortgage. I went to work at a foster care agency working with at-risk children. Other jobs might have paid more, but this one gave me the opportunity to make a difference in the lives of children.

I might have stayed in that job until I retired if Sue and I hadn't sat on the couch one Saturday night to watch a little television. My story would have had no less of a happy ending. Our life was good. Very good.

And it was about to change forever.

24
It All Comes Down to This

The carnival atmosphere that marked the beginning of the heads up showdown between Tuan Lam and me didn't last long. People get tired, even in Las Vegas. Most of the observers in the grandstands around the feature table had been there since play had begun fourteen hours earlier.

I was exhausted. At this point, adrenaline alone kept my body running. With my huge chip lead, I thought I could end this quickly. Final head-to-head matches at the main event rarely last longer than ten hands. None of the last three had lasted longer than seven.

Then again, none of those final tables had featured Tuan Lam. His style of play defined patience.

Norman Chad, ESPN's color commentator during its broadcasts of the World Series of Poker, said that Tuan Lam had folded his way to the final table. That is not too far from the truth.

I don't mean this as a criticism of Tuan's strategy. Far from it. Any strategy that takes you to the final head-to-head show-down in a tournament that began with over 6,000 players is a good one.

In fact, Tuan had been an aggressive player through much of the tournament. Going into the final table, he took a different approach. I knew he could be a tight player, but I didn't realize how tight.

Of the seven players who'd been sent home thus far, I'd knocked out six. Tuan, not a single one. He'd taken to heart John Kalmar's idea many hours earlier that he could sit back and let me take everyone's chips, then face me head-to-head. John had busted out a long time ago, but Tuan was still very much in contention for poker's biggest prize.

I had a four-to-one chip lead, yet both of us were well aware that Philip Hilm had held a three-to-one chip lead on me at one time before becoming the first player to bust out.

The first dozen hands between Tuan Lam and me primari-ly consisted of one or the other of us folding before the flop. Only three hands went all the way to the river, including the very first. Even on those that progressed past the flop, the pots remained small. I could not lure Tuan into risking any of his chips beyond the bare minimum.

My legs and shoulders ached. Not only had we been playing for over fourteen straight hours, but we'd played over sixteen hours on day six and fourteen hours on day five.[9] On top of the physical strain, each of those days had been filled with emotional leaps and letdowns. I planned to sleep for about a

---

9. This was the last year all seven days of the main event were played consecutively. Beginning in 2008, the final table would take place in November while the rest of the tournament would still be played in July.

week once this was finally over.

When the cards were dealt on the fourteenth hand of our head-to-head showdown, I thought, *This is it. This will end it.* I was the first to act, which is advantageous for an aggressive player, especially with a hand. And I had a hand. "Two point six million." I was already in the pot for $600,000.

He called.

The flop came: king, queen, six.

We both checked.

The turn card came: five of clubs.

Tuan bet 3 million.

"I'm all in," I said in response. Those words woke up the crowd. *Come on, call,* I said in my mind over and over. *Just call, and let's end this. Now!*

Forty-five long seconds passed.

Finally, without saying a word, Tuan slid his cards toward the dealer, giving up the hand.

We had to keep playing.

The next eight hands consisted of more limping into the pot and folds. I took seventeen of the first twenty-one hands and in the process cut Tuan's chip stack in half. Yet I couldn't deliver the knockout punch. The few times he made a large raise or went all in, I didn't have the cards to call. The last thing I wanted to do was double him up.

Tuan made his first big mistake on hand 23, which was hand 192 of the final table. He was the first to act and pushed all in.

You must keep in mind that Tuan had played tight all

night. However, when a player finds himself on the short stack, he will often push all in from the button as a way of stealing the blinds and antes, thus buying a little more time. I suspected that was exactly what Tuan was trying to do.

I held an ace-ten, so I called.

As soon as I did, I knew I had him. He pulled off his glasses and pursed his lips, which was a sure sign he was bluffing. I flipped over my cards, and his expression seemed to say, *Uh-oh*.

The moment he turned his cards, I knew why. He'd gone all in with a puny three-four off suit, one of the top ten worst hands in Texas Hold 'Em.

I pumped my fist in excitement while the crowd behind me went nuts.

Then came the flop. King. Eight. *Four*.

My heart sank. The Canadians in the crowd woke up and cheered like crazy, waving flags and chanting. Honestly, not much had happened the past hour. Everyone in the stands had been waiting for a reason to bust loose.

The hand was far from over, but I knew it didn't look good for me. I had to hit an ace or a ten to take both the pot and the tournament.

The turn card was a six, the river a king.

Not only did I double his chip stack, but I gave him a shot of confidence and made him believe he wasn't dead yet.

Tuan proceeded to take four of the next five hands. The pots were tiny in comparison to the number of chips in play, but that didn't matter. He came to the final table determined to wait me out, no matter how long it took. His strategy had always been to bide his time, play strong hands, and pray for lucky breaks. He caught one when I doubled him up. A couple more, and he might well win the whole thing.

A full dozen hands passed. Tuan Lam and I had now played twice as many hands in the final head-to-head showdown as there had been in the previous three main events combined. I still had over 100 million in chips. Tuan had 25 million, still only slightly more than he'd had when play had begun at noon.

Hand 205. The clock neared four in the morning. I was on the button, the first to act. I looked at my cards. Pocket eights, the same hand I'd had when I'd first taken the chip lead and the same hand that had knocked out Alex Kravchenko.

I stared at those eights. As I look back at this moment, I think about the day my family climbed on the bus to leave Ban Vinai for America. The camp authorities placed us on bus eight. Over the previous week and a half of poker, pocket eights had kept me alive when I'd been on the brink of busting out, and they'd pushed me up the chip ladder time after time. What a welcome sight they were now.

"I raise." I slid 2.3 million into the pot.

Tuan flipped some chips in his hand for a few moments. He looked at his cards. Ten seconds passed. Fifteen. Twenty. Finally, he said, "I'm all in."

I immediately knew what I wanted to do, but still I waited.

From the background, someone yelled, "Do it."

I had doubled up Tuan once already; I didn't want to do it again. Yet if ever I was going to knock him out, this was my chance. "I call."

The moment Tuan saw my cards, he stood up, threw his cards faceup on the table, and yelled, "Yes!"

He was not bluffing this time. He held an ace-queen of diamonds, the sixth strongest hand in Texas Hold 'Em.

Once again, the crowd woke up. The noise was deafening, Canadians cheering on one side, Americans on the other. The carnival was back. Flags waved. People chanted. I know it was only poker, but from where I stood, it felt like the Olympics. The way the crowd carried on, this was nation against nation, the United States versus Canada, with national pride on the line.

Tuan egged on the Canadians, amplifying the noise in the Amazon Room.

Me? I prayed, just as I had on every big hand.

The flop came. *Queen*, nine, five. He paired his queens and immediately became the odds-on favorite to take the hand.

No, not again. I remembered a story I'd heard about the final table of one of the first World Series of Poker championships. It had lasted something like *three days*. When that queen hit the table, I thought, *Oh, God, I don't know how much more of this I can take.*

Tuan had the exact opposite reaction, as you'd expect. As soon as he saw the queen, Tuan grabbed a Canadian flag and waved it, cheering.

I just prayed that much harder.

The dealer burned a card, then laid down the turn card. A seven. At first the dealer's thumb covered part of the card, and I thought it was an eight.

No such luck.

However, the seven quieted the Canadian side of the room just a bit. That little card, along with the five and nine that hit on the flop, gave me a chance for a gut shot straight. It wasn't a good chance, but I would take it. Out of the forty-five cards potentially still in the deck, the two eights and four sixes would give me the hand and the championship. If any of the other thirty-nine hit the table, Tuan and I would keep playing.

"It's okay," Tuan, still confident, yelled to his supporters.

Believe me, if I'd been in his position, I would've felt confident as well.

I picked up the photograph of my children that I'd kept with me since the first day and held it close to my face. That photograph had kept me grounded. Every time I looked at it, I knew what I was playing for. *Oh, God, give me the grace to handle whatever happens.*

It was time for the river.

Of the four sixes in the deck, one decided to come out and play. I made my straight!

Just like that, my life changed forever.

Almost two years to the day earlier, I had pointed at ESPN's broadcast of the 2005 World Series of Poker and announced to my wife, "I can do this. And when I win, I will use the money for good."

At ten minutes till four on a Wednesday morning in Las Vegas, I wrapped my arms around my wife as poker's world champion.

I hadn't done this. We had done it. Together.

Postscript
The Heart of a Champion

In an interview immediately following my victory over Tuan Lam at the final table, Norman Chad of ESPN said to me, "You've said the day you came to America from a refugee camp in Thailand was the greatest day of your life. How does this feel?"

I suppose the answer most people expected would have been something like, "Oh, this day is even greater." After all, it isn't every day you're handed over $8 million in cash. And those millions were sitting right there on the table next to me. But I couldn't compare winning this title to that day. I simply couldn't.

"That was the happiest day of my life. Winning the World Series of Poker also means a lot to me because I know I can use this money to do a lot of good."

I took those words seriously. I wouldn't be able to look in the mirror if I didn't live them out.

Of course, that doesn't mean I gave all the money away or

felt guilty when I spent some on my family and myself. Not at all. We did use part of the money for ourselves. My newfound wealth allowed my wife to quit her job so she could stay at home with our children, as she'd always wanted. We no longer have a car payment or a mortgage payment. Right after my victory, we sold our house in Temecula and moved closer to both our parents' homes.

However, neither my wife nor I regarded the wealth as a license to indulge our every desire. Both the title and the prize money I took home from Las Vegas that day represented a great responsibility.

I have read many stories of people who fall into wealth only to blow it all in a short time and end up even poorer and deeper in debt than they were before the windfall. Using my winnings for good meant investing them wisely, making them last for the rest of my life as well as the rest of my children's lives. How could I live with myself if I did otherwise?

I also believe the title of World Poker Champion lays a great responsibility at my feet. Many people automatically assumed that as world champion, I would turn pro. They expected to see me on the poker circuit full-time. I seriously considered the possibility and almost did it, but after much prayer I came to believe that God had a different plan.

I still play tournament poker, including many World Poker Tour events. However, I primarily play charity events where I can use my celebrity to raise money for causes near and dear to my heart. I have also worked to bring other poker players and celebrities aboard. For me, using my title for good means helping change the lives of others, not adding to my own personal bankroll.

Not everyone believed me when I vowed to use my winnings for good. I encountered a great deal of skepticism over it.

People said, "Come on, Jerry, let's get real. Do you honestly expect me to believe you're going to give away one-tenth of the $8.25 million you just won?"

I guess they thought I'd said it only to look good on camera. My response was always the same: "Of course I'm serious. This will be the first check I write . . ."

Even before my victory, I knew which causes I wanted to support, in addition to my local church and some local charities I had been involved with.

When my wife and I decided where we should give this portion of my winnings, the choice seemed obvious.

Part of the money went to the Make-A-Wish Foundation. During my graduate work at Loma Linda University, I'd spent a great deal of time working in the hospital. There I'd seen children with no hope of recovery. I'd also seen the hope and joy Make-A-Wish gave them. Having grown up around so much death, so much hopelessness, I thought, *If this group can bring joy to a dying child, I want to support them.*

Another part of the money went to the Ronald McDonald House. I became acquainted with this organization, too, while in graduate school. While volunteering here, I spoke with many parents who had no other place to stay while their children were in the hospital. The Ronald McDonald House was making a tremendous difference in the lives of children and their families. Even as a graduate student, I knew someday, if I were able, I wanted to do something to help this work grow.

Beyond giving the organization a one-time gift from my winnings, in September of 2009 I launched the annual Jerry Yang Celebrity Poker Tournament at the Tachi Palace Hotel & Casino in central California specifically to raise money for the Ronald McDonald House near my home.

Another portion of the 10 percent of my prize money went to a work I had long been familiar with. Back in 1992 while in college, I'd awakened in the middle of the night and couldn't go back to sleep. After tossing and turning a while, I got up and turned on the television and immediately knew why I was awake. There on my television was a man named Larry Jones, the president of an organization called Feed The Children, along with his crew, passing out food to children in a refugee camp in Zambia.

I knew those children could have been me.

I pulled out my checkbook and wrote a check for $30, also including a note that said something like this: "Dear Mr. Jones, thank you for your work with children. I'm only a college student and don't have much money, but I want to support your work. Please take this $30 and use it for the children. Someday I hope to be able to send more." I sealed the letter and the check in an envelope and went back to bed at four in the morning.

A couple weeks later, I received a nice note signed by Larry Jones thanking me for my gift and telling me it was people like me who made the real difference. I never forgot that letter.

Over the next few years, I'd sent checks to Feed The Children as often as I could. I also did a little research on the organization and found that Larry Jones had consistently operated with integrity and the highest levels of accountability. He was the real deal.

After winning the 2007 World Series of Poker, I called Larry and talked with him for a while. Out of that conversation, I decided that instead of simply writing a check, I wanted to underwrite a Feed The Children food drop in Southern California. On the day of the drop, I would help pass out the food right out of the backs of the semitrailers. I couldn't wait.

As the day of the food drop approached, I did a little more research, made some phone calls, and did some digging on the Internet. That's when I discovered that Larry Jones' Feed The Children had brought food and clothing into Ban Vinai, the refugee camp where I'd lived four years. They had helped feed and clothe me when I was one of the starving children in a Third World refugee camp.

When I was in high school, the woman who paid my tuition asked me to promise to show the same kindness to others that I had received. This is now my life's mission. It's why I fulfilled my vow to use my winnings for good and why I live the way I do today. The highest calling is not to someday be the best or the brightest in your chosen field. No, it is to use one's life for good.

Whatever you have, whether a lot or a little, use it for good.

That is the mark of a true champion.

Appendix
Jerry's Winning Poker Strategies

Someone once said poker is a game you can learn in an afternoon, but it takes a lifetime to master. Truer words have never been spoken. Even though I'm a World Series of Poker champion, every day I realize how much more I have to learn. What follows is a small part of what I've learned thus far through both experience and from the books and advice of players I deeply respect. I hope they will help you as you work to master the wonderful game of Texas Hold 'Em.

8 Things Beginning Players Need to Know

1. Play to win. Anytime you sit at the table, you should play with the determination to come out on top. Playing to win is different from playing cocky. The former means you'll exercise the patience, discipline, and determination to prevail. The latter means you'll think, *I can beat all these bums with one hand tied behind my back.* Cocky players usually lack the patience to wait through hours of bad cards for a good hand. You need to be confident in your abilities without dismissing the others' skills.

2. Learn the game. Read books by great players. Watch instructional videos. Study televised tournaments. Do everything you can to learn strategies and the subtle keys to success. Remember: it takes a lifetime to master poker.

3. Don't quit your day job. Poker may look simple on television, but winning consistently is difficult. Even the best pros go through dry spells, losing far more than they win. If you take it up, do it for the love of the game, not because you're sick of your current career. Who knows? You may have what it takes to make a living at it, but every pro will tell you making this a career demands extremely high levels of commitment, focus, and the willingness to grind away at the table day after day.

4. *Never risk money you can't afford to lose.* First and foremost, take care of your family. Pay your bills. Pay your mortgage. Put groceries on the table. Only then can you set aside extra money for a bankroll for entering tournaments. When you do enter a tournament or buy into a cash game, look at that money as the price of admission. If you win it back and more, you will have had a great day. But if you lose it, you will have still had a wonderful time playing a game you love. This attitude allows you to play with greater patience and discipline.

5. *You must be patient.* Winning consistently comes down to knowing when to apply pressure to your opponents. It's all about waiting for the right moment to strike. Well-timed aggression takes pots and wins tournaments.

6. *Know yourself.* Good players prey upon the weaknesses of their opponents. You need to know your own strengths and weaknesses, both as a player and in your personality. Understand your own emotional makeup. You can't control your opponents' actions, but you can control your reactions.

7. *Concentrate.* This should go without saying, yet I find many players are only interested when they have a stake in a hand. The moment they fold, they pull out their phone and begin texting or checking their e-mail. I tell all my students to keep their focus completely on the game. Don't let your mind wander. Watch at all times, especially when you're out. Pay

close attention to how your opponents play each hand. The information you gather will help you later.

  8. Control your emotions. All is fair in love and war . . . and poker. More than once, I've found myself at the table with a player who does everything he can to get under my skin and put me on tilt. I've had players criticize my abilities and even my habit of praying at the poker table. If I let those players get to me, I will soon lose. Always keeping emotions in check is especially difficult when you endure a bad beat. Remember, they're part of the game. Everyone loses from time to time due to the luck of the draw. That's poker. You can't lose your temper or become frustrated when someone hits a gut shot eight high straight on the river and beats your three aces. Accept the bad beat for what it is, and wait for the perfect opportunity to win back your chips.

Top 8 Rookie Mistakes

This book is not long enough to list all the rookie mistakes I made in my first tournament. I finished in the money that day, which proves only one thing: even the worst players get lucky from time to time. Early success often proves to be a curse for beginners because it can reinforce bad habits, but I made careful notes from my first experience and did my best to master the basics. What follow are the eight most common rookie mistakes every player must correct to achieve long-term success.

1. Playing too many hands. Experienced players know they must fold many hands to survive long enough to take advantage of a strong hand when the cards fall their way. Rookies don't understand this. They call and raise and stay in nearly every hand because of the mistaken belief that everything in poker comes down to the luck of the draw. Successful players create much of their own luck by knowing when to stay in a hand and when to walk away.

2. Lack of patience and discipline. Poker on television appears to be a nonstop stream of drama and intrigue. That's because ESPN never shows the endless string of hands when everyone folds to the big blind or someone makes a quick raise to which everyone else drops out, giving him the blinds and antes. At this stage in a tournament, monotony and boredom can push people into playing bad hands and making rash decisions. You must be patient to win. You must also keep your emotions in check as you make your way through strings of bad luck and bad beats. Without discipline, you're doomed to fail.

3. Bluffing too much. Every player bluffs from time to time, projecting strength when, in fact, they have nothing. However, the more you bluff, the more the other players at the table will figure you out and begin setting traps for you. In the end, you become the boy who cried wolf, and your fate will be similar.

4. An overinflated ego. The Bible says pride comes before the fall. That is especially true in poker. Many beginning players live in denial and mistakenly believe their skills are greater than they actually are. An early run of luck, like the one I had in my first tournament, often feeds the ego and makes the player think he can beat anyone. You must be humble to succeed in poker. If you believe you can step up and run a table, beating everyone with ease, you'll soon find yourself going home with empty pockets.

5. Not knowing when to step away from a game. I see this all the time. A player loses in a bad beat. He becomes angry and determined to get even no matter what. Suddenly he starts taking unnecessary risks, all because his emotions have taken over. If you reach this point, you need to get up from the table, gather yourself, and come back when you can be patient and disciplined.

6. *Consuming alcohol while playing.* Hollywood portrays a successful gambler sitting at a table, a glass of whiskey in one hand, cards in the other. That may make a good movie scene, but it doesn't work in the real world. Alcohol and drugs affect your emotional state and your decision-making ability. Success demands that you stay as sharp as possible, which is why I tell all the players I coach to avoid alcohol completely while playing.

7. *Playing too long.* Most amateurs play too many hours at a time, going from cash game to cash game until fatigue takes over and they lose their ability to concentrate. I also see this when players lose in a tournament and immediately go to the cash games to try to recoup their losses. This is a bad idea because they start in a bad place emotionally. The end result is an even greater loss to their bankroll.

8. *Risking more money than you can afford to lose.* When I play poker, I always leave my ATM card, credit cards, and extra cash at home, where they're safe and sound. Never use money for poker that you need to pay bills or buy food. When I started out, I set aside extra money each week, the same amount I would have spent in greens fees if I'd taken up golf instead. On the weeks we needed that money, for example, for an unforeseen medical bill, I didn't play. When money is tight, content yourself with playing poker with your friends and family at home, betting matchsticks or pennies. This is a game you should play for fun and relaxation. Good money management is the key to long-term success.

Top 8 Tells

Success in poker comes from playing your opponents as much as, if not more than, you play the cards. Part of playing your opponents is the ability to pick up on a tell, or a physical reaction, behavior, or habit that tells you something about a person's hand. Tells can let you know when a player is bluffing or when he has a very strong hand. Understanding the most common tells also helps you cut off the flow of information you may give to other players about your own hand: information they plan to use against you!

Here are the eight tells I watch for the most. Keep in mind that other players often fake these as a way of laying a trap for an unsuspecting player.

1. The speed with which a player makes a bet. If a player tosses his chips very fast onto the table, that usually represents weakness. Conversely, if he calmly moves his chips in, that usually signifies strength.

2. The distance between the player and the chips he bets. When a player throws his chips far from his body, this is usually a sign of intimidation and a weak hand. Usually, he does this in an attempt to intimidate the other players, as if he's so confident in his hand that he cannot control his excitement. I have found that most players who toss their chips a long way from themselves usually have a weak hand. Those who slowly move their chips right in front of them usually have a strong hand.

3. Pursing or tightening the lips. Pay close attention to a player's mouth when he makes a bet. If he licks his lips, tightens them, or purses them, he is probably bluffing. This nervous twitch is hard to control, even for the best players. I even saw it in my opponents at the final table of the World Series of Poker.

4. Crossing the feet. When you're at the poker table, pay close attention to the posture of those sitting on either side of you when they're first seated. If they're relaxed but then cross their feet and sit up more when they make a big bet or go all in, it's often a sign of bluffing.

5. Fanning the cards far apart. This is usually a sign that your opponent does not have a pair and that the cards in his hand are not suited.

6. Flipping cards quickly. If, when your opponent picks up his cards, he takes a quick look and then flips them back down, he probably has a very good hand. You don't need to study a pair of kings or aces for a long time to figure out whether you'll call, raise, or fold. However, you do when you have jack-ten off suit.

7. A change in the way a player taps the table when checking. If your opponent normally taps the table softly two or three times, then in one hand taps it harder or taps five or six times, it's a sign he doesn't have a hand. Instead of checking, you should fire back at him with a quick raise.

8. Twitching. A player who sits calmly when placing a bet probably has a good hand. However, if his neck or hands twitch, it's a sign of nervousness, probably over a weak hand.

Top 8 Hands to Play

You can find books and Internet sites that give the odds of success for every possible two-card combination you will encounter in Texas Hold 'Em. I find it easier to play by this simple rule of thumb, especially in the early rounds of a tournament. I play pocket pairs from eight and up, along with ace-king suited.

Again, that is:

Pocket 8s

9s

10s

Jacks

Queens

Kings

Aces

Ace-king suited

In the early rounds of a tournament or the early stages of a cash game when I have very little information about my opponents, I play tight. That means, I usually fold unless I have one of the above hands.

Basic Tournament Strategy

Whether you're one of the more than 7,000 players competing in the main events of the World Series of Poker or you've entered a charity tournament at your local casino, you need to prepare yourself to succeed. The following basics helped me on my way to my World Series of Poker victory.

The night before the tournament begins
Get plenty of rest. Relax as much as possible. Meditate. Pray. Go to bed early.

The worst thing you can possibly do is play in a late-night cash game before the tourney begins or spend a couple of hours at the blackjack table while you wait for the tournament to begin. You wouldn't go out and challenge your neighbor to a footrace the night before running in the New York City Marathon. In the same way, you shouldn't expend the energy you'll need for a big tournament in a small cash game the night before. Do whatever you must to be as fresh as possible when you sit down for the first hand of the tournament.

In the tournament early stages
Learn everything you can about the other players at the table. Ask them where they're from, what they do for a living, how long they've been playing poker. Then, once the cards are dealt, make mental notes about the players, their betting patterns, whether they play tight or overly aggressively. Information is power, and you want to gain all the information you can about your opponents while trying to give away as little as possible about yourself.

Play tighter than normal. Don't be reckless. Only play premium cards. Play your position and pick your opponents carefully. In the first round you can't win the entire tournament, but you can certainly lose it.

Work to position yourself for later rounds. Your goal at this stage is to accumulate chips. You don't have to be the chip leader, but you want to put yourself in a position of strength for the later rounds, not barely hold on with a short stack.

Middle rounds
In the middle rounds, you move from playing your cards to playing your opponents. Use your position at the table and choose your opponents carefully based on the information you've gathered thus far.

Loosen up and become more aggressive. As the blinds increase, to survive you have to start taking more chances. You must be patient, but if you fold every hand, you will soon run out of chips.

Final stage

Prey upon the short and medium stacks. In the latter stages of a tournament, most players are content to simply cash out. Therefore, you can apply more pressure to those who are thrilled to have simply survived this long.

Use the information you've accumulated thus far. Review your notes on the players you'll now face, especially when you make it to the final table.

Watch out for desperate players. You don't want to double up those who have nothing to lose. Use your position on them and answer their aggression with even more when you have a strong hand.

Play looser, but don't go all in with stupid hands. If you have a large chip stack, don't become cocky and try to throw your weight around. You must remain patient and disciplined.

If you have the short stack, play your position to take as many blinds and antes as you can. Don't go all in against those who have so many chips they can afford to call you at any cost. Time your moves carefully, but be aggressive. If not, the blinds alone will soon take away your stack.

Don't play to merely cash out. Play to win.

Acknowledgments

I would like to thank the following people:

First and foremost, my wife, Sue, for your continual support throughout my early years as an amateur poker player and for believing in me. During the last sixteen years of marriage, you have been there for me every step of the way. You are the foundation of our family. To my six children, Beverly, Justice, Brittney, Brooke, Brielle, and Jordan, for your love and patience. Your prayers have given me the strength to be the best father I knew how and to play poker to the very best of my ability, giving me the strength to be patient, persevering, determined, and courageous when I've needed to be.

To my father and mother for your understanding and unconditional love and support. Dad, you are my teacher, provider, counselor, and hero. Without you, I would have been dead somewhere in the jungles of Laos or one of the refugee camps in Thailand. To my older brother, Cher Xay Yang, and sister-in-law Mee Her for loving and supporting me like a son.

To my parents-in-law, Fai Teng Khang and Vue Yang, for your undying support, guidance, and teachings. I couldn't have asked for a better father and mother-in-law. To my Grandmother Pla Her and Aunt Mee Yang for your love and support when I was young.

To Mark Tabb, for the tremendous number of hours you spent crafting the book so beautifully. Thank you and your wife for being so hospitable and generous while we spent time in your home working on the book. Thank you for your kindness and your skill in putting the story together.

To Noah Vang for providing invaluable photos for the website. And to those who donated photos to Noah, thank you.

To Lee Hough and his team at Alive Communications for your professionalism, your representation on my behalf, and your continual support.

To the whole team at Medallion Press for the opportunity to publish my book and for your generosity and support.

—*Jerry Yang*

Thank you, Jerry Yang, for entrusting me with telling your story. I value our friendship that developed while working on this book.

Thank you, Helen Rosburg, for your enthusiastic embrace of Jerry's story. You told me you wanted this book for Medallion Press the moment you first heard about it. Helen, you are a woman who knows how to make things happen. Just thinking about you puts a smile on my face. I appreciate you more than you can know.

Thank you, Emily Steele, and the rest of the editorial team at Medallion for your patience and your persistence.

Finally, a special word of thanks to my wife, Valerie. Thank you for putting up with my psychotic deadline self.

—*Mark Tabb*

MEDALLION
P R E S S

Be in the know on the latest
Medallion Press news by becoming a Medallion Press Insider!

<u>As an Insider you'll receive:</u>

• Our FREE expanded monthly newsletter, giving you more insight into Medallion Press

• Advanced press releases and breaking news

• Greater access to all of your favorite Medallion authors

Joining is easy. Just visit our website at
<u>www.medallionpress.com</u> and click on the Medallion Press Insider tab.

MEDALLION
P R E S S

Want to know what's going on with
your favorite author or what new releases
are coming from Medallion Press?

Now you can receive breaking news,
updates, and more from Medallion Press
straight to your cell phone, e-mail, instant messenger, or Facebook!

Sign up now at www.twitter.com/MedallionPress to stay on top of all the
happenings in and around Medallion Press.

For more information
about other great titles from
Medallion Press, visit
m e d a l l i o n p r e s s . c o m